Chris Sprague's
NEWCASTLE INN COOKBOOK

December, 1996

To: Jean and Tim

Thank you both so very much for sharing in our experience.

All my best,

Chris

"The Inn at Ormsby Hill"

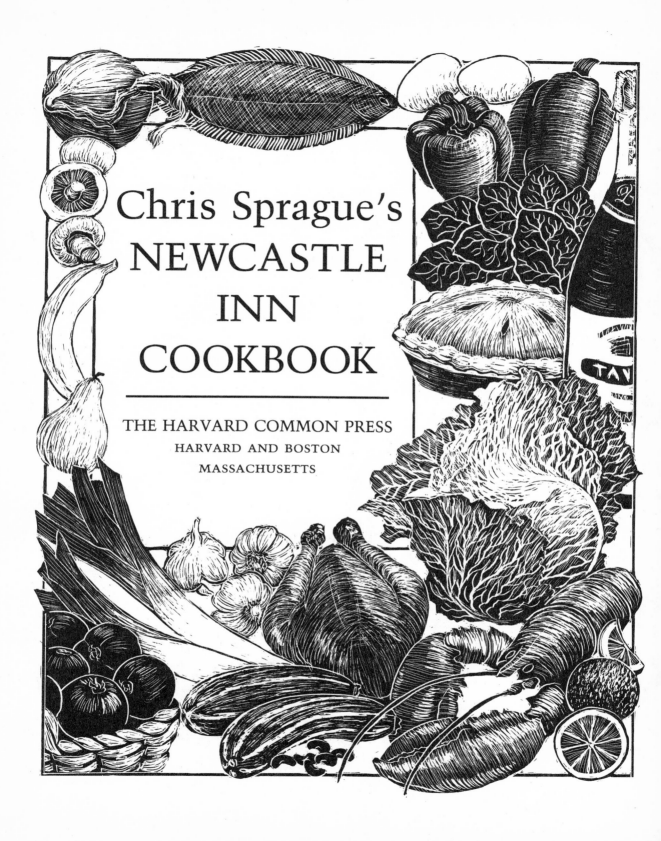

Chris Sprague's
NEWCASTLE
INN
COOKBOOK

THE HARVARD COMMON PRESS
HARVARD AND BOSTON
MASSACHUSETTS

The Harvard Common Press
535 Albany Street
Boston, Massachusetts 02118

Printed in the United States of America

LIBRARY OF CONGRESS CATALOGING-IN-PUBLICATION DATA

Sprague, Chris
Chris Sprague's Newcastle Inn Cookbook : recipes
and menus from a celebrated New England inn /
Chris Sprague.
p.   cm.
ISBN 1-55832-050-4. — ISBN 1-55832-049-0 (pbk.)
1. Cookery, American.   2. Cookery, European.
3. Menus.   4. Newcastle Inn (Newcastle, Maine)
I. Title.   II. Title: Newcastle Inn cookbook.
TX715.S7596   1992
642'.4—dc20   92-21366

Front cover photograph by Charles Freiberg
Author photograph by Doug Mindell
Cover design by Joyce Weston
Scratchboard illustrations by Joanna Roy
Text design by Linda Ziedrich

10   9   8   7   6   5   4   3   2   1

FOR

My grandmother, who would be so proud of me,

My father, from whom I learned my love of food, and

My husband, Ted, for helping make my dreams come true—
this book is as much yours as mine.

CONTENTS

ACKNOWLEDGMENTS

I owe gratitude to many people who are very special in both my personal and professional lives, and who have supported and encouraged me. I truly apologize to anyone I may have forgotten here.

Heartfelt thanks—

To Lucy Wheaton, our adopted grandmother. We will never forget the first day we met her, eighty-five years young, walking down the hill with her ski pole, bringing cookies to welcome us. She arrived as we had all the brochures we had ever collected spread over the living room floor, trying to design our own. She spent three hours with us that day, telling us stories about our inn. Lucy was our inn-sitter the first year we owned the inn, and our guests absolutely adored her.

To Mimi Steadman, to whom I will be forever grateful for her tireless attention to detail and *all* her invaluable advice— I couldn't imagine asking anyone else to be the first reader of my manuscript—and for her friendship. Working with her is always a special joy. And to her husband, Rick, for never saying no to a dinner invitation.

To Bill Oates and Heide Bredfelt, for their wisdom, guidance, and expertise.

To Cynthia Hacinli, Maura Curley, Ken Gouldthorpe, and Kathy Gunst, for writing such wonderful things about us.

To all the inn-book writers and travel writers who have reviewed our inn. Where would we be without them?

To so many innkeepers, and to Joanne Bell, Pat Hardy, and Wendy Denn of the Professional Association of Innkeepers

International, for being inspiring examples of passion and professionalism.

To Don Johnson and Esther Cavagnaro, for being so caring and for telling so many people about us.

To Bev Davis and Rick Litchfield, for generously sharing their knowledge, and for being friends, mentors, and examples of perfectionism.

To those who supply me with the best of ingredients: Scott Simpson and his family from Simpson's Seafood, Bambi Jones from Hidden Valley Farm, Jan Gorenson from Gorenson's Farm, Don Thompson from Windward Farm, Deirdre Barton and Joanne Lewis from Weatherbird, Ralph York, Fred Trani, and Bob Cloutier. Thanks also to Diane Gimbel from Gimbel Gardens, for always helping make us look so good. And to everyone at Coastal Business Center, for meeting all our rush deadlines.

To Craig and Dolores Foster, for their support and friendship, and for trying to make sure that we take some time to smell the roses. And to Jack Lynch, for his guidance and wisdom.

To Ugli Endler, Goldilocks Westerman, Sharon Schermerhorn, and Diane Kenney, for their friendship over the years.

To all the guests who have given us so much support and encouragement, without whom we could never have come this far.

To our entire staff, both past and present. Without them, nothing would have been accomplished.

To my parents-in-law, Kay and Wesley, for all their love and support.

Finally, to Ted. For his sense of humor when I needed it most, I give him my greatest thanks, love, and appreciation.

INTRODUCTION

I AM OFTEN ASKED where I studied cooking. My honest answer is that I am not a trained chef and I have never taken a cooking class. I am completely self-taught. I am just a person who truly enjoys cooking and making people happy.

This is the story of how my husband, Ted, and I became innkeepers, and how I became known for my cooking at the Newcastle Inn.

I was born and raised in Lynn, Massachusetts. In my childhood and early adulthood I was surrounded by good food. When my grandfather came from Greece, he started a small grocery store in Lynn, and when my father returned from the war, he went into business with my grandfather. The store, which changed location four times, evolved from a typical small grocery into a well-known gourmet food store.

I started working at my dad's store at a very early age, after school and weekends. I learned a lot in those years, both about food and about serving the public.

My mother was an excellent cook, but because I worked with my father in the store I never cooked a thing as I was growing up. Then one Saturday my dad asked me if I would like to cook us dinner for that evening. I asked him what he would like, and he said that he'd like a real quiche Lorraine. I went home, found a recipe, went back to the store to gather all the ingredients, and went home and made a quiche Lorraine with a crust from scratch. For dessert I made a triple-layer Boston cream pie. Boy, was I proud of myself. I realized then, when everyone loved the dinner and gave me great praise, that cooking was for me.

I started cooking often for my family and friends. Later on I did small catering jobs and ran a very small baking business out of my home.

Ted was born and raised in the small town of Hinsdale, New Hampshire. His parents had a small farm, and just about everything they ate they raised—beef, pork, and vegetables. Ted's mom even churned her own butter. So Ted learned when very young what really fresh food tasted like. Years later, when Ted and I had our own vegetable garden, I learned this, too. There is nothing like picking fresh peas from the garden, shucking them (while trying not to eat all of them raw), cooking them, and having them for dinner—all in an hour's time.

Guests often ask me where my recipes come from. I have a very large cookbook collection, and I read every cooking publication I can. I can tell just by looking at a recipe if it will work for me. By making a couple of changes, I make the recipe mine. Most new recipes, after all, are just adapted from old ones.

I am also asked if I experiment on Ted and myself before I serve a dish to our guests. Absolutely not! I tell our guests all the time that I experiment on *them*. When I make my rounds of the dining room during dessert, I tell our guests if a dish is new and ask their opinion of it.

I have made this a book of menus to correspond to the way we serve dinner and breakfast at the inn. We serve everyone the same meal, in five courses at dinner, so it made sense to organize the cookbook this way. But there is no reason why you have to follow my menus. Feel free to create your own.

I often hear guests say they could never cook a meal as I do. I tell them that they can definitely do it, if they can read and if they enjoy cooking. After all, these are my only qualifications.

Why We Decided to Become Innkeepers

This is one of the questions we are most frequently asked.

When Ted and I were first married, we spent our first Columbus Day weekend at a bed-and-breakfast in North Conway, New Hampshire. I vividly remember how I felt there. I loved being cared for in someone's home, and meeting people from all over the country. "When I grow up," I told Ted at breakfast, "I want to be an innkeeper."

Whenever we traveled after that, we always stayed in an inn or bed-and-breakfast. We visited North Conway every fall to hike and see the foliage, staying in a variety of places.

In 1986, when we both became disenchanted with our occupations (Ted a high-school chemistry teacher, I an office manager in a law firm), we started thinking about what we would enjoy doing instead. I loved cooking, entertaining, and decorating. Ted loved gardening and renovating (by this time Ted had built our three-bedroom Colonial garrison house on Cape Cod, and we had a huge vegetable garden). We were both homebodies. We loved the weekends, not just because they were breaks from work; we truly loved being at home doing the things we liked.

It seemed natural for us to become innkeepers.

The Search for Our Inn

We contacted a real estate agent on Cape Cod who told us of two inns for sale in nearby Brewster. We knew them well. One we loved tremendously, but the price was too high, considering all the work it needed.

The second inn had a four-star reputation for dinners, and six guest rooms upstairs, which shared two baths. We could put in private baths, we thought, and build living quarters for ourselves. We made an offer, but the owners turned it down. (In six months they would come back and offer us the inn for $100,000 less than we had offered them!)

We then went to an innkeeping seminar led by Bill Oates, from Brattleboro, Vermont. One of the main things we learned from this seminar was that a chef could own you. What if on Christmas Eve the chef says that if you don't give him a $10-per-hour raise he will walk out the door? I said to Ted, "I can do the cooking." The inn that hosted the seminar served everyone the same dinner at the same time. If we did likewise, and set a reasonable limit on the number of guests, I could certainly manage it.

By the end of that seminar, we knew we had made the right decision to become innkeepers. We hired Bill as our consultant, and went to work looking for our inn. I wanted one in Vermont; Ted preferred New Hampshire. But we would be happy in either state.

We thought about how we would run our inn. During a two-week vacation we stayed at thirteen different inns, visiting others along the way and talking with many wonderful innkeepers who were happy to share their stories. We filled out a questionnaire on every inn we visited, noting what we liked and didn't like about each one.

The first inn we visited, near North Conway, was for sale. When we drove up the driveway we both felt it could be ours. We loved the location. The view of the mountains was incredible.

After our two-week trip, we made an offer on the New Hampshire inn, and it was accepted. We found a buyer for our home on the Cape. I spent two weeks cooking dinners at the inn; we ordered living-room furniture and wood for the winter; and we knew which employees were staying.

Then one morning Bill Oates called to say that the bank had approved our financing. We were really going to be innkeepers! I called Ted's school and asked the clerk to interrupt his class so I could tell him the good news. We were both on top of the world.

Ten minutes later a Federal Express truck pulled up. I didn't know what the truck might be bringing, but I had a feeling that it would not be good. It turned out to be a letter from the bank for the buyers who were purchasing our house. The buyers, the letter said, did not qualify for their loan. I cried hysterically. Without the money from the sale of our house we couldn't buy our inn. I called the school and asked the clerk to interrupt Ted again. We had never gone from such a high to such a low so quickly.

We tried everything we could think of to save the inn purchase (including trading our house to the innkeepers) but nothing worked. We had to give up the inn.

All of these events occurred between early September and late November of 1986. To say that Christmas of 1986 was our worst is putting it mildly. Ted was even more depressed than I; mentally he had left teaching. In my heart, though, I knew there was a reason the sale hadn't happened—that inn was not meant to be ours.

We waited for our home on the Cape to sell before we began our search again. Then we found an inn in Vermont we liked, but the owners decided not to sell. We were running a streak of bad luck.

Bill had told us about inns in Maine a couple of times, but neither Ted nor I wanted to be in Maine. When the Newcastle Inn went up for sale, we decided to go see it to prove to Bill that we did not want to be in Maine. When we drove down the River Road and saw the inn, I said to Ted, "This is not my inn; I am not going to live here." But after spending the night we decided that if we could move the building to Vermont, we could be really happy.

We called Bill and told him we didn't want the Newcastle Inn. Two weeks later he asked us to spend two days at the inn with him, to look at it more closely. He said that every new innkeeper has to make a compromise, and ours might have to be location. So we spent a couple of days with Bill at the inn, and tried to make a decision. Ted was more than ready to be out of teaching. I told him that if he really wanted to buy this inn, I would go along. After a lot of discussion, we made an offer to purchase the Newcastle Inn.

When we had begun searching for an inn, Ted and I planned to make a ten-year commitment to the one we found. But when we decided to purchase the Newcastle Inn, we agreed that we would stay for only three years, fix it up, sell it, and move on to our next inn.

Two weeks after we bought the inn we made our three-year plan a five-year plan. Two months after that we made our five-year plan a ten-year commitment. We had fallen in love with Maine. We had found our home.

The Inn

We wouldn't even show our families and friends photos of the inn when we purchased it because it needed so much work. I was embarrassed; I wanted it to be perfect right away. It was not one of those beautifully decorated inns you see featured in magazines.

The inn had nineteen guest rooms, most with shared baths. Our first project was to reduce the number of rooms to fifteen and put in all private baths. We hired a crew to do most of this work, since we needed to concentrate on learning to become innkeepers, developing our marketing strategies, and so on.

Since that first year of major remodeling, Ted has done all the subsequent renovations. We have made a lot of changes, although we are still waiting to make others. But we have come a long way and are very proud of where we are now.

So where are we? Newcastle, Maine, is the twin village to Damariscotta. The two villages sit on opposite banks of the Damariscotta River, connected by a small bridge. (An Indian word, *Damariscotta* means "meeting place of the alewives," which are a type of herring.) We are halfway between Freeport and Camden and a twenty-minute drive north from Boothbay Harbor.

This is where you explore life as it should be. Take in the fishing harbor scenes; visit the ancient oyster shell heaps along the Damariscotta River; see the lobster boats in John's Bay and the little villages; take a drive down to Pemaquid ("long finger") Point to see Pemaquid Lighthouse, one of the most photographed in Maine. From the Pemaquid Peninsula, take a boat over to Monhegan Island.

This is a wonderful place for Ted and me to live. We have a real sense of community. There are no fast-food franchises, no malls, no neon signs—just a small coastal village. Tourists don't congregate here; we are not overwhelmed in peak season. We know that if we were in one of the busier towns in Maine we would be doing a much higher volume of business—but we would not be happy living in one of those towns. The way of life we've found here is definitely more important to us than making a lot of money.

Our First Guests

I can't imagine there are innkeepers who cannot remember their first guests. Ours?

We purchased the inn on December 18; our first guests were to arrive on Christmas Eve. We spent the days between cleaning, rearranging, and decorating for Christmas. On Christmas Eve the tree was lit, and there was a welcoming table with candles, homemade eggnog, and all my traditional homemade Christmas cookies. We were excited and proud. At eight o'clock Ted and I were sitting in the living room, with a roaring fire in the fireplace, starting to feel a little panicky. No one had checked in yet. Was there a mistake? Was no one coming?

At nine o'clock a young couple came to the door, and we both jumped up to welcome them. They had no reservations but needed two rooms for the night, one for them and one for their parents. They told us they were in the area to share Christmas with their family in Boothbay. They were headed to Boothbay to spend the remainder of the evening, and would come back to the inn to spend the night. They would leave early the next morning to have breakfast with their family.

The two couples left quietly on Christmas morning. We were sorry they couldn't have experienced our first breakfast, with the other guests who had finally checked in the evening before.

A few hours after they left, one of our housekeepers presented us with a bottle of champagne and a note, both of which she had found in a guest room. The note read:

Dear Ted and Chris,
    We love your new home! Best wishes and continued success on your new adventure. You have a beautiful place and you are the type of people who will make the Newcastle Inn a special place. It already is special to us.
                    Merry Christmas,
                    Bob and Barb Grinnell

That Christmas evening, while having dinner alone and sipping the champagne, we had tears of joy. We had truly made the right decision to become innkeepers. We couldn't imagine ever being happier than we were at that moment.

The Rabbits

Another question we are frequently asked is, Why the rabbit logo and all the rabbit images?

Because I was born on Easter Sunday, my family has always called me Bunny. When I was working at my dad's store, all the customers called me Bunny, too, because that was the only name they knew me by.

The first year Ted and I were married, he bought me little figurines of a mother rabbit and her three babies. This started my rabbit collection. Whenever we would travel we would always buy one special rabbit figurine, and others we would buy just because they caught my eye or Ted's.

When we purchased the inn, we knew our logo had to be a rabbit. A local artist, Jane Pitts, drew our now very familiar rabbit logo.

Over the years our guests have given us many more rabbits to add to our collection. All are very special and have found homes somewhere in the inn.

The Bloomer, who sits at our front desk, is my favorite rabbit figurine. When Joel Bloom, whom I used to work with, came to visit us with his wife, Susan, for the first time, they presented us with Bloomer. The Halls and Paralikases, who visit on New Year's Eve, have started their own rabbit collection at the inn. A Japanese restaurateur who had never stayed at an inn before sent us an adorable stuffed "sleeping" rabbit after she returned home to Japan. And Rick Litchfield traded me his antique rabbit doorstop for one of my father-in-law's duck decoys.

The rabbits that are closest to our hearts come from Ted's mom and dad. Mom has made us beautiful rugs, including the first one she ever hooked. For Christmas of 1991, she made us a rug that has our logo in four corners and "Newcastle Inn" across the middle. Another rug she made also has bunnies, and a footstool she covered for us bears the rabbit logo. Dad has made two rabbit-topped walking canes.

The most special rabbit in the inn is a club that one of Dad's friends made. Dad had dug the root, but could not make a face or figure out of it. He gave it to his friend Robert Simmons, who brought it back a few weeks later to show Dad the rabbit he had created. Dad told Bob that his daughter-in-law would love to see it, and brought it here on one of their visits. I thought it was absolutely wonderful. About a week before Bob died, he gave the club to Dad. On one of our visits to see Ted's parents, Dad presented me with it. This was a gesture of love that brought tears to his eyes and mine.

Finally, there is one rabbit I can't live without—the rocking-rabbit toy that Ted gave me for our second Christmas as inn-keepers.

The Start of Dinner Service

We did not begin serving dinner until May 1988. Before we could start dinners, we had to learn to become innkeepers. We learned to prepare and serve food by starting with breakfasts.

Our breakfasts have always been special. We felt they had to be something that our guests would not normally make for themselves. Our guests started spreading the word about our breakfasts. Now, whenever guests tell someone local that they are staying at the Newcastle Inn, the subject of breakfast always comes up. When we added dinners in 1988, our reputation for them started immediately, partly because we were already known for our good food.

Because we had spent so much money refurbishing the inn before we started serving dinners, the budget was tight. We used old china that we had found in the basement (it was not bad, actually) until we could replace it—half in 1990 and the remainder in 1991. We also used the silver included in the purchase, until we finally bought new flatware in 1992.

We knew we wanted a small, very select wine list. That first year we started with just California wines. We have since doubled the size of the list and added wines from Europe, but the list is still small and select. Because Ted and I are not wine connoisseurs, we rely heavily on the experts.

We did a lot of work researching food suppliers, and we're happy with the results. All year round we get our fish fresh in Wiscasset. We have eggs and milk delivered weekly, and our produce man regularly goes to Boston for fresh produce. Our specialty foods also come from Boston.

In the spring, summer, and fall, Bambi Jones and Jan Goren-sen raise all our vegetables and some of our fruits. I love working with them; they raise absolutely beautiful vegetables. Sometimes they grow special crops, like fennel, at my request. I get so excited when I see the first crop of anything—beans, lettuce, asparagus, raspberries, or herbs.

I even have a man growing hydroponic lettuce and some herbs for us during the winter months, so our green salads are always a picture.

I am fortunate in that everything, except for the fish, is delivered to our door. Especially during the busy months, it is almost impossible to run any errands, let alone go out each day to purchase food supplies.

Deirdre and Joanne from the Weatherbird (our local gourmet food shop) are a wonderful source. Whether for cheeses or any special foods I may need, or for unusual items they may want me to try out on our guests, or when I have questions about anything, they always have the answers.

I knew that serving dinner would mean hard work and long hours. I also knew that the most important catchwords would be *service, service, service*. These things have held true both for serving dinner and for everything else about running the inn.

A Typical Day

Some of our guests want to know what my day is really like. They may see me only at the end of their dinner, when I am dressed in my visiting clothes (not the soiled ones I cook in all day), wearing lipstick. And they have this wonderful, romantic vision that they too could do this.

What they don't realize is that my day starts by 5:30 in the morning. For my mental and physical health, I walk three and a half miles every day with Destiny, my dog. Then, during the off-season, I prepare breakfast for our guests. (In 1991 we hired someone to cook breakfast six mornings a week from June through the end of October, the months when we also serve dinners every night.)

My mornings are spent talking with guests, doing paperwork, working on advertising and marketing, taking care of any housekeeping problems, arranging flowers, and ordering, receiving, and putting away food supplies. Sometimes I may prepare a dessert or some dinner dish that requires an early start, but for the most part I do not do much food preparation in the morning.

I try, every day that I can, to take a thirty-minute nap at noon. My nap gives me the energy to put in my long hours.

I start cooking every day at one o'clock. An assistant works with me—five days a week in July and August, and an average of three days a week in June, September, and October. (The rest of the year the inn serves dinner only on the weekends and for private parties.) My assistant and I spend the afternoon doing all the prep work for dinner, and baking the bread for breakfast the following morning.

During the summer and fall months, when our local produce is at its peak, we do extra cooking to fill the freezers for the winter months, when really fresh produce is hard to find. We make a lot of soups for the freezer (asparagus and pea, sorrel, arugula, red and yellow pepper bisque, to name a few). We also make breakfast breads with ingredients available only certain times of the year (blueberry cake and raspberry streusel are two favorites).

To keep our energy high, we play rock music continuously between one o'clock and five o'clock. But as soon as the wait staff arrives at five, off the music goes. There is too much else going on.

Between five and seven is "roller-skating time," as I tell my assistant. I start to panic, thinking I am never going to get everything done on time for dinner—although I can think of only once when we had to seat guests late.

When the wait staff comes in, they set the tables, get the greens ready for salads, and perhaps wash some dishes. When the guests start arriving at six, our waitresses begin taking cocktail orders, serving hors d'oeuvres, and, if necessary, matching couples to share tables in the dining room.

Between six and nine, things seem absolutely crazy in the kitchen. But the dinner is like a ballet, perfectly choreographed in every way. I get out course after course, making sure everything is served promptly and hot. I time the courses and tell the waitresses when to clear and when to serve. Ted, meanwhile, opens and pours all wines, helps to fill the plates, dresses the salads (I'm a lousy dribbler), carves or slices the meat, slices the frozen desserts—*and* manages to answer the phone and check in late-coming guests.

Our guests are never rushed during dinner; they have time to savor the course they have just eaten. Dinner at our inn is like an elegant meal in someone's home.

As our guests are having their entrées, Ted and I sit down and eat our dinner—not in a very leisurely fashion, unfortunately. I then run to change into my visiting clothes. While the guests are eating their desserts, I walk around the dining room and chat with them. Those who have come for the night I welcome to our home. I enjoy these visits, which are usually my first opportunity to talk with our overnight guests. Others have come just for dinner; I enjoy greeting them, too. It is always gratifying for me to see all those smiling faces and receive all those compliments.

The only time during the day that I have a chance to sit down is when I handwrite the menu cards for dinner. Bedtime for me is usually ten-thirty—later if we have a lot of guests.

Our Guests

The very best reason for doing what we do is to meet and share experiences with people from all over the world. For us, our guests are an extension of our family. So, we make our inn a special experience for them. We answer their letters and questions, and we respond to their complaints. We pamper them. And they truly appreciate it all.

Karen and Kirke, who stayed at our inn when they first became a couple, have been back several times. Three years after their first visit, they have decided that they can't imagine having their wedding anywhere but at our inn. I can't wait to make this event perfect for them.

Mike Odell once asked us to serve the whole dining room champagne one morning at breakfast so that everyone could help him toast Kelly, his wife, on their anniversary.

Craig and Dolores, after purchasing and renovating their summer home near our inn, bought our first bottle of Roederer Cristal Champagne, only to share it with us to celebrate their move. We became such good friends that, when I told Dolores I couldn't find a bandana for Destiny, she quickly offered to help. The bandana Destiny now wears used to belong to Craig.

I could fill a book with stories like these. Although we are the ones providing a service, our guests give us a lot in return.

Words are hard to find to explain the emotion we feel every time we receive a thank-you from a guest. Our guests will search for that special rabbit card on which to write a thank-you, or for that perfect little rabbit figurine to give us when they check out. Sometimes they will even go home and make a rabbit for our collection. I remember the guest whose husband, having stayed here once on business, brought her for their anniversary. He had told her about the rabbits, and she arrived with one for our collection. She knew before she came that she was going to love being here.

When our guests Joel and Susan Bloom came to the inn, they wrote us a poem, which they presented to us on the last night of their stay:

NO ROOM (FOR IMPROVEMENT) AT THE INN

If you would like to stay quite thin,
Don't dine at the Newcastle Inn.
When you call up and speak with Ted,
Tell him you're eating out instead.

Because my friends, I'll tell you this:
You've never met the likes of Chris.
She has one goal in life, I've found,
To fill her guests until they're round.

Imagine if you will a stay
That starts with Roquefort cheese soufflé.
And that's the *first* course, not the main,
To guarantee a large weight gain.

A soup, a salad, biscuits, too—
These courses serve to lead up to
A complex main course. With some luck,
She'll stuff you too with breast of duck.

We're staggered by these great delights,
But Chris still has us in her sights.
We're near the shore, we limp toward port—
Oh lord, a chocolate truffle torte!

(And just to show that she's the boss
She tops it with strawberry sauce!)

We give, we yield, we're done, we're sated!
It's all that we anticipated.
Five nights of culinary best
Have spoiled us now for all the rest!

And so dear Chris and so dear Ted,
We're awfully glad that you two wed,
And bought this great Newcastle Inn,
So we could come and feel like kin.

Joel and Susan Bloom

Our greatest satisfaction of all comes when guests give us big smiles as they leave and tell us they can't wait to come back.

Our Staff

I am not an easy person to work for. My standards, as well as our guests' expectations, are high. I expect perfection in service and in every detail. The shades have to be at certain heights, the curtains just so, the tables and chairs a certain way, the pictures absolutely straight, and so on.

I tell our wait staff that a guest could have the finest dinner he or she has ever eaten, but if the service is less than excellent, that is what the guest will remember most. I will not allow a guest to feel slighted in my dining room.

Fortunately, we have an incredibly responsible, dependable, and dedicated staff. They treat guests in our inn as they would treat visitors in their own homes. It is gratifying to see one of our staff welcome back a repeat guest, or for repeat guests to remember the same housekeeper or waitress who served them on their last visit. For the guest, it is like coming home.

People love the special attention our staff give them. A waitress might remember that a certain guest likes tea instead of coffee and might bring the tea before the guest has even asked for it.

When I make my rounds in the dining room, I always get

compliments on our staff. They have really made us what we are today. We could not do what we do without them.

The Food

The best adjective I know to describe my cooking is *simple*. There is nothing complicated, nothing fancy about my food. No wild combinations of flavors, no fussy presentations. My meals are simply well prepared and soul-satisfying.

In my cooking, I do not use hard-to-find ingredients. Since we are an hour away from Portland, and three hours from Boston, I do not have the time to spend shopping. I don't mind, though. The quality of the ingredients, not their rarity, is the critical element in the success of a dish. We use only the best and the freshest of foods.

I do spend a lot of time cooking. Because we serve everyone the same thing at the same time, I can make time-consuming dishes that restaurants generally cannot. For example, we often serve risotto. I stand at the stove for 35 to 45 minutes just adding liquid and stirring. One minute away from the pot will cause the rice to burn. Guests who know how risotto is made are thrilled when they see it on our menu. I make soufflés, too, for both first and dessert courses; they always get rave reviews. Most of our soups take a lot of work, and so do some of our unusual breakfast breads.

Every evening at seven, we serve a five-course dinner—first an appetizer, then soup, then salad and cream biscuits, then the entrée, and finally dessert. I have left the recipes for our salad dressing and biscuits out of the book because they have been our trademarks since we started serving dinners. Some things are hard to let go of, and these two recipes are among those things.

But it is to the desserts that I devote the most time and energy. Desserts, especially those made with chocolate, are my first passion. I sometimes spend hours just making the dessert. But when I walk through the dining room each evening and look at the guests eating my desserts, those smiles, those looks of sheer ecstasy, tell me the results are well worth the effort.

When I cook, it is as though I am giving a dinner or breakfast party. Every meal is special. I never think about how hard or how time-consuming something is to prepare; I just make it. I never think about the fact that I don't have a substitute in case of an emergency. Probably if I had had professional training I would have a different attitude. Thank goodness I don't know any better.

There *have* been failures. There was the morning when I attempted to make oatmeal popovers. I put into the oven all the little custard cups filled with the oatmeal mixture. Our mouths watered as we waited, anticipating big, airy popovers, ready to be split open and spread with butter. The timer went off. I opened the oven door. What we found in the custard cups was a cooked mixture that rose only halfway up the sides. We had nothing to substitute, so we served the popovers with butter and jam and called them oatmeal muffins. Everyone loved them. But we never tried that recipe again.

Then there was the morning I couldn't remember how much flour I had put in the mixture for baked pancakes. The batter seemed a little runny, so I added an extra cup of flour. Instead of rising to a beautiful top-hat shape, the pancakes came out like little firm bowls. We served them as lemon pancakes rather than baked pancakes, and no one knew otherwise.

In four years of serving both dinner and breakfast, these have been my only two disasters in the kitchen.

There is one thing about my meals that brings some negative comment. I am known for my large portions. I can't help this; it's my heritage. Ted has been trying for years to get me to reduce portion sizes, and I have—just a little.

I have learned a lot since I first started serving dinner. I never worried about experimenting on our guests, but I have become more daring, gutsier. I am also concentrating more on balancing flavors and textures in my menus. Guests notice this—that the first course flows into the second course, that the flavors complement one another. Guests who have eaten with us since 1988 say that every year they can see a definite change in my cooking, that it keeps getting better.

We do not skimp on quantity or quality of ingredients, on labor, or on anything else. We take great pride in the food we serve.

The Accolades

I never imagined that my passionate interest in cooking would bring our inn such recognition, and in such a short period of time.

September of 1989 brought us our first restaurant review; Cynthia Hacinli of the *Maine Times* gave us three stars.

October of 1989 brought a feature on us in *Down East* magazine under the heading "Pampering Places—Country Inns Where the Cuisine Rivals the Felicity of the Accommodations."

On March 11, 1990, we were reviewed in the *Maine Sunday Telegram*. We will never forget that date. On the first of March I received a telephone call from Maura Curley, the paper's restaurant reviewer. She asked if a photographer had been to our inn to take pictures. "What for?" I asked, surprised. She then told me that a review of our dining room would appear the following Sunday, and that she'd like to ask me questions about the dinner she had had. As she was going through the menu, I looked through my dinner book and found that she had been here two weeks earlier, on a Friday. I remembered that was the evening I had dropped a pan cover on the floor of the kitchen, while the door to the dining room was open. The cover rolled around a couple of times before I could stop it. The noise was *so* loud. Then Ted clapped, and I was truly humiliated. I figured two stars for service.

When she was through asking questions, I asked her if she could tell me how many stars we were going to receive. She told me she couldn't; I would have to wait ten days for the review. It was the longest ten days I have ever spent.

Since we had received three stars from the *Maine Times* a year earlier, I was hoping for three and one-half stars. Ted said he would be happy with three.

On Sunday morning, March 11, Destiny and I took our usual walk. When we got back I hurried to our quarters to see if Ted had brought the newspaper. On the door was taped a sheet of paper with three rows of four stars. I walked in and said to Ted "Yeah, sure. What is it really?" He showed me the four stars—the highest rating a restaurant could receive—in all three categories. I never cried so hard.

On Saturday evening, March 10, we had had two guests for dinner. Ted and I had served them ourselves in the living room in front of the fireplace. On Sunday, March 11, our lives changed completely. After that review appeared, we had a full house of twenty-four for dinner most weekends. People drove long distances just to come for dinner.

For the first two weeks after the article was published I was nervous cooking dinner—I felt I was on display. I knew I must never make a mistake because people were expecting perfection, a four-star experience. I finally calmed down and realized that as long as I kept doing what I had done in the past I would do just fine.

We thought nothing could top the *Maine Sunday Telegram* review until we were featured in *Food and Wine* magazine. This time we knew in advance that a reviewer was coming; we found out at two o'clock on an afternoon in July 1989 that a writer from *Food and Wine*, and his wife, would be having dinner at our inn that evening and spending the night. It was too late to come up with a special menu for the occasion. I was a wreck.

Dinner and breakfast went fine, though. Ted and I spent some time talking with Ken Gouldthorpe and his wife, Judy. Ken was researching an article on the southern coast of Maine for the magazine's travel section. If the magazine was going to run the story, he said, he would be back for another visit.

It was over a year later that Ken called to say he would be coming back in a week. I planned a menu very different from the one we had for his first visit—salmon rather than pork, lemon-layered ice cream cake rather than chocolate truffle torte, capellini rather than a soufflé.

The article finally came out in May 1991. The Newcastle Inn, Ken wrote, was "exactly what a small country inn should be." The phone started ringing; we had calls for reservations from all over the United States. One couple came all the way from California just for a weekend with us.

More flattering reviews followed. David and Linda Glickstein of *The Discerning Traveler* said the "Newcastle Inn fits our image of everything that we look for in a full service inn. . . . We give The Newcastle Inn our vote for one of the finest meals we've had in Maine."

In March 1992 *Yankee* magazine did a twelve-page article

on our inn and my food. Although the New England economy was weak, the article helped make 1992 our best season yet. And because the photographer had found Destiny to be very photogenic, everyone who has visited because of the *Yankee* article just can't wait to meet her.

We tell our guests that we have been incredibly lucky. They tell us that luck has nothing to do with our success—that it is all due to hard work and a love for what we are doing.

What Sets Our Inn Apart from Others

The first thing that sets us apart from most other inns is the food.

The second is our attention to details. Our guests notice everything, and it is the little things that mean a lot. When someone is celebrating a birthday, we serve dessert or coffee cake with a candle in it, on a handmade plate bearing the words "Happy Birthday to You." For anniversaries, honeymoons, and other occasions for congratulations, we use a red plate that reads "You Are Special Today." When a couple were celebrating their fiftieth anniversary with us, we decorated their room with yellow roses, yellow ribbons, and a huge bouquet of yellow balloons. When we turn down the bed covers at Easter, we put a white chocolate and a dark chocolate bunny in the middle of the pillows with a card with the guests' names on it, wishing them a happy Easter from the Easter Bunny.

The third and probably most important thing that sets us apart is how we make our guests feel, when they call and when they are here. Ted is a perfect host; his relaxing, easy manner and sense of humor make everyone feel welcome and at home. My kitchen door is always open while I am cooking breakfast, and our guests feel comfortable coming in and talking with me while they are seeking out that first cup of coffee. But I especially love when repeat guests, who know I am behind those closed kitchen doors cooking dinner, will stop in, give me a hug, and say hello before finding Ted and their rooms. They know that if I can chat for a few minutes I will.

The last thing that sets us apart are our special celebrations. These are some of the most popular:

Thanksgiving: We serve a six-course dinner at one o'clock, and leftovers and pies in the evening—just like at home.

New Year's Eve: With a classical guitarist, seven courses, and a champagne toast at midnight, this is our most popular celebration.

Valentine's Day: Roses, chocolates, candles, and champagne greet guests upon their arrival.

Cooking with Chris Weekend: This is a hands-on class, in which we prepare dinner for all the evening's guests. The class is usually held in March.

Mutual Benefit Weekend: We draw five previous guests' names from a hat and invite the winners for a dinner and a one-night stay at no charge, but with a catch. They have to spend two hours on Sunday morning telling us ways to improve our inn.

Birding Weekend: Ted and well-known local birdwatchers take our guests to favorite and little-known spots.

Monhegan Adventure: The weekend stay includes a full-day trip to Monhegan Island.

Hike and Windjammer Weekend: This favorite weekend includes a morning hike up Mt. Megunticook in Camden, with a beautiful view of the coast of Maine, and a windjammer cruise in the afternoon.

Some Last Thoughts

I received my first standing ovation just three weeks after we started serving dinner. I thought everyone in the dining room was applauding a local businessman who was celebrating his birthday. When I told him how wonderful I thought it was that they were doing this for him, he said, "Chris, look around, they're doing it for you." I had never experienced such emotion. I couldn't believe this was happening to me. I still get goosebumps thinking of it.

I have told Ted many times, especially in the first few years, that I sometimes felt as though I were on the outside looking in—as though the incredible things happening to us were really happening to someone else while I just watched. It has often seemed that the praise and the gifts of thanks couldn't possibly be for us.

We were sure that becoming innkeepers would not make us wealthy, but wealth is measured differently by different people. Ted and I have never wanted monetary wealth. Our wealth is in our way of life and in all the people we have come to know. We knew when we became innkeepers that we were giving up everything—our home, our jobs, and seeing our old friends. Our only regret is that we didn't do it sooner. Ted and I followed our dreams; we are living out our fantasy.

I truly love what I do, and I want to share my joy with you in this book.

For reservations or further information about our inn, call or write Ted or me at the Newcastle Inn, River Road, Newcastle, Maine 04553; (207) 563-5685.

BREAKFAST

OUR FAVORITE BREAKFAST

Sour Cream Coffee Cake

Apple Crisp

Individual Baked Pancakes

THIS IS OUR FAVORITE BREAKFAST because it reminds us of the past. Simple and satisfying, sour cream coffee cakes have been around forever. Apple crisp makes us feel warm and cozy, like well-nurtured children again. It's real "comfort food."

The baked pancake is truly our favorite, for several reasons. First, it is the lightest of the breakfast entrées we serve our guests. It is also the easiest one to make. And, finally, it is the most spectacular of breakfast entrées. This is what you serve when you really want to impress someone. When we make baked pancakes in our special pans, they look like top hats. I love standing in the kitchen and listening to the sounds coming from the dining room while the wait staff serves them. Mostly I hear laughing, and the question "How do we eat it?" Just pour a little maple syrup into the center and dig in!

Frank and Brinna Sands, the owners of King Arthur Flour, tasted our baked pancakes when they stayed with us on the way to their summer home. At their request a year later, I contributed this recipe to the *King Arthur Flour 200th Anniversary Cookbook*. King Arthur has always been the only kind of flour I use.

Sour Cream Coffee Cake

Sour cream coffee cake never goes out of style, and I think it is still the most delicious of breakfast cakes.

2 cups all-purpose flour
1 teaspoon baking powder
1 teaspoon baking soda
Pinch salt
½ cup (¼ pound) unsalted
    butter, at room
    temperature

2 eggs
1½ cups sugar
1 cup sour cream
1 teaspoon vanilla extract
½ cup chopped walnuts
1 teaspoon ground cinnamon

Preheat the oven to 350°.

Grease well and flour a 9-inch tube pan.

Sift together the flour, baking powder, baking soda, and salt.

Cream the butter with 1 cup of the sugar until light and fluffy, approximately 5 minutes. Add the eggs and beat until blended. Add the flour mixture in thirds, alternating with the sour cream and ending with the flour mixture. Add the vanilla, and mix until just blended.

Combine the remaining sugar, the walnuts, and the cinnamon in a small bowl.

Pour half the batter into the tube pan. Sprinkle half the nut mixture over the batter. Repeat with the remaining batter and nut mixture.

Bake for about 45 minutes, until a toothpick inserted into the center comes out clean. Cool in the pan for 10 minutes before removing the cake. Cool a bit longer before slicing. Serve warm.

Serves 8

Apple Crisp

This apple crisp is great served warm from the oven with a small scoop of vanilla ice cream. There is no law against serving ice cream for breakfast—our guests will certainly attest to that!

6 large tart apples, preferably Granny Smiths
1 tablespoon lemon juice
½ teaspoon ground cinnamon
¼ teaspoon ground cloves

¾ cup all-purpose flour
½ cup sugar
½ cup light brown sugar
6 tablespoons unsalted butter, cold

Peel, core, and slice the apples. Toss the slices with the lemon juice, cinnamon, and cloves. Place the apple mixture in a shallow two-quart non-aluminum baking dish.

Preheat the oven to 350°.

With an electric mixer on low speed, blend the flour and the sugars. Cut the butter into 12 pieces, and add it while mixing. Stop the mixer once the mixture starts to clump.

Sprinkle the topping evenly over the apples.

Bake until the topping is lightly browned and the apples are tender, approximately 40 minutes.

Serve warm from the oven or at room temperature.

Serves 6

Individual Baked Pancakes

These pancakes, served directly from the oven, are impressive in shape and size. The *oohs* and *aahs* from the dining room always make me smile. I can't tell you how many times guests have run to their rooms to get their cameras.

3 eggs	Pinch salt
½ cup milk	2 tablespoons unsalted
½ cup all-purpose flour	butter, melted

Whisk the eggs with the milk until well blended. Add the flour and the salt, and whisk well. Add the melted butter, and whisk well again so that the batter is smooth.

Grease two 6-inch round cake pans, unless they are the nonstick kind. Pour the batter into the pans.

Bake in a preheated 450° oven for 15 minutes. Quickly turn the pancakes out of their pans, put them right side up, and garnish them. Serve them immediately while they are still tall.

GARNISHES:

We usually serve these pancakes with lemon zest and lemon juice sprinkled over the middle, and confectioner's sugar dusted over the tops. Guests top them off with our Maine maple syrup.

You might instead sprinkle sliced strawberries over the middle, then dust confectioner's sugar over the tops. Sautéed apples also go nicely with these pancakes. Try other fruits, too, depending upon the season.

I usually serve these pancakes with sausage links.

Serves 2

THE BETTER HOMES AND GARDENS BREAKFAST

Blueberry Lemon Bread

Strawberries with *Crème Fraîche*

Ricotta Cheese Pies

WE WERE THRILLED when we were asked to submit recipes for *Better Homes and Gardens'* new cookbook. We were one of only five inns to be featured, with six pages of recipes and a color photograph.

This was the first time we worked with a professional photographer, and what a learning experience it was. The team spent an entire day with us, adjusting the lighting, arranging the furniture, and choosing among cameras and lenses for each shot. I think the hardest time they had was when they tried to photograph Ted and me. We are not the most willing subjects in front of a camera, anyway, but in addition they just did not like the clothes I had picked out, or the way we looked in our dining room. After four wardrobe changes, we sat for the photographer on the stone wall in front of the inn with Destiny beside us. This photograph was chosen for their cookbook, *Better Homes and Gardens Recipes from Country Inns and Bed and Breakfasts*. The photo is truly one of our favorites.

We have been preparing this breakfast menu since we first started serving breakfast, and it is one of our guests' favorites. I hope it will brighten a summer morning for you.

Blueberry Lemon Bread

There are more wild blueberries in Maine than in any other state, and their harvest and marketing is a very important industry here. We use blueberries in many ways, but this bread is one of our favorites, for its simplicity both in preparation and taste.

6 tablespoons butter, softened
1 cup sugar
2 eggs
1½ cups flour
1 tablespoon baking powder
¼ teaspoon salt
½ cup milk
1 cup fresh blueberries
1½ tablespoons grated lemon rind
1 teaspoon lemon juice

Preheat the oven to 350°. Grease and flour a 7½-by-3¼-inch loaf pan.

In a large bowl, cream the butter and the sugar. Add the eggs, and mix.

Sift together the flour, baking powder, and salt. Add dry ingredients a little at a time to the butter and egg mixture, alternating with small quantities of the milk, and stirring constantly. Stir in the blueberries, lemon rind, and juice. Turn the batter into the loaf pan, and bake the bread 50 to 60 minutes, or until a cake tester inserted in the center comes out clean.

Serves 8

Strawberries with *Crème Fraîche*

Crème fraîche is sold in most supermarkets. If you can't find it, use my simple recipe.

Fresh strawberries, hulled   Brown sugar
Crème fraîche (recipe
    follows)

For each serving, place three to six strawberries upright in a small bowl. Place 1 heaping tablespoon *crème fraîche* on top of the strawberries, in the center of the bowl. Sprinkle brown sugar over the *crème fraîche* and berries.

FOR THE *CRÈME FRAÎCHE*:
1 cup heavy cream   ½ cup sour cream

Whisk the creams together in a small bowl. Pour the mixture into a jar, cover it, and let it stand in a warm place for 12 hours. Stir the *crème fraîche*, and refrigerate it for 24 hours before serving.

Makes 1½ cups

Ricotta Cheese Pies

These unusual pies can be prepared ahead for ease in serving. Phyllo (or filo) dough is available in the freezer sections of most supermarkets. Many people think that using it is difficult, but if you work quickly and take care not to let the dough dry out, you will forever be a fan of phyllo.

Mascarpone cheese is available in specialty food shops. If you can't find it, substitute cream cheese.

½ pound mascarpone cheese, at room temperature
3 egg yolks
15 ounces ricotta cheese
⅓ cup sugar
Zest of 1 large orange, grated
1 tablespoon vanilla extract

1 tablespoon Grand Marnier liqueur
½ pound phyllo dough, thawed in the refrigerator
½ cup (¼ pound) unsalted butter, melted

With an electric mixer, beat the mascarpone cheese and egg yolks until smooth. Beat in the ricotta, sugar, orange zest, vanilla extract, and Grand Marnier, and continue beating just until the ingredients are blended.

Place one sheet of the phyllo dough vertically on a work surface (keep unused sheets covered with a dampened towel so they don't dry out). Brush the sheet generously with the melted butter. Place 3 heaping tablespoons of the cheese mixture in a line across the lower center of the sheet. Fold up one-third of the phyllo sheet, fold in each of the sides, then fold over until you have a compact package.

Repeat this procedure for each pie.

Place the finished pies seam-side-down on a baking sheet. If you wish, you can refrigerate the pies overnight.

Preheat the oven to 375°.

Brush the tops of the pies with the remaining melted butter. Bake them until they are golden brown, about 15 minutes.

Sprinkle the pies with confectioner's sugar, and serve them with slices of ham.

Serves 12

NOT YOUR USUAL FRENCH TOAST BREAKFAST

Orange-Poppyseed Cake

Baked Stuffed Pears

Grand Marnier French Toast

THIS MENU IS FOR A SUNDAY MORNING, or any morning you can spend at leisure—a not-a-care-in-the-world morning. This could also be for a special-occasion breakfast—just add a bottle of champagne, or perhaps mimosas.

The poppyseed cake is one of the first breakfast cakes we served, and it still is one of our guests' favorites. They have requested this recipe more often than any other. They have even begged to purchase whole cakes from the freezer.

I usually serve simple poached pears for breakfast, but I thought we needed a change—and what a change these pears are.

The elegant french toast, with or without maple syrup, is X-rated—it is definitely not for children.

If you have suffered too many mornings of toast and coffee on the run, you'll enjoy treating yourself to this extra-special breakfast.

Orange-Poppyseed Cake

This is a not-too-heavy and incredibly moist cake. I hope you enjoy it as much as our guests have.

1½ cups (¾ pound) unsalted butter, at room temperature
2 cups sugar
6 eggs
¼ cup finely grated orange rind
¾ cup poppyseeds

1 teaspoon vanilla extract
2¼ cups all-purpose flour
1 teaspoon baking powder
1 teaspoon baking soda
½ teaspoon salt
1 cup milk, at room temperature

FOR THE SYRUP:
⅓ cup orange juice   ¼ cup sugar

Preheat the oven to 350°. Grease well and flour a 10-inch loose-bottomed tube pan.

With an electric mixer, cream together the butter and sugar until light and fluffy (about 2 minutes). Add the eggs, orange rind, poppyseeds, and vanilla, and beat for 2 minutes. Stir together the flour, baking powder, baking soda, and salt. Add the dry ingredients to the butter-sugar-egg mixture in three parts, alternating with the milk in two parts. Beat well after each addition.

Pour the batter into the tube pan, and bake about 60 minutes, until a cake tester inserted in the center comes out clean. Cool the cake on a wire rack for 10 minutes. Remove the outer side of the pan, leaving the bottom and center of the tube.

In a small bowl, stir together the sugar and juice until the sugar is dissolved. Spoon the sugar mixture evenly over the cake.

Remove the cake from the tube when it is completely cooled.

Serves 12

Baked Stuffed Pears

These pears are wonderful for breakfast and could even be served as a simple fruit dessert by just adding a scoop of vanilla ice cream while they are warm.

½ cup hazelnuts
¼ cup dried sweet cherries
¼ cup Frangelico liqueur
6 pears, preferably Anjou or
  Bartlett, ripe but still firm

¾ cup confectioner's sugar
½ teaspoon vanilla extract

Preheat the oven to 350°. Place the hazelnuts in a single layer on a baking sheet. Toast the nuts 15 minutes, or until they turn golden brown. Let them cool, then chop them fine.

While the nuts are toasting, put the cherries with the Frangelico liqueur in a small bowl. Let the cherries soak for 15 minutes. Drain the cherries, reserving the liqueur.

Set the oven to 375°. Peel, halve, and core the pears. Arrange them in a single layer in a shallow baking dish.

In a bowl, combine the cherries, sugar, hazelnuts, and vanilla extract, and mix well. Fill the pear halves with this mixture. Pour the reserved Frangelico liqueur over the pear halves.

Bake the pears for 15 minutes, or until they are tender. Serve them hot or cold with some of the cooking liquid spooned over.

Serves 6

Grand Marnier French Toast

I prefer to serve this adult version of french toast without maple syrup, but Ted always puts syrup on his.

6 eggs	1 teaspoon ground cinnamon
¼ cup Grand Marnier liqueur	4 tablespoons unsalted butter
2 tablespoons maple syrup	1 1-pound loaf challah bread, cut into 12 thick slices
2 tablespoons heavy cream	Confectioner's sugar
1 teaspoon finely grated orange peel	Orange slices

In a large bowl, beat the eggs, Grand Marnier, maple syrup, heavy cream, orange peel, and cinnamon with a wire whisk until smooth.

Melt 1 tablespoon of the butter in a large skillet over medium heat. Dip four slices of challah bread into the egg mixture until they are well saturated. Sauté them in the butter, turning once, until they are golden brown on both sides, approximately 5 minutes. Transfer them to a warm serving platter, and keep them warm.

Repeat with the remaining challah bread slices, adding more butter as needed.

Divide the french toast among six plates. Sprinkle the tops generously with the confectioner's sugar, and garnish with orange slices.

I serve sausage patties as an accompaniment.

Serves 6

HEARTY WINTER BREAKFAST

Carrot Cake

Bananas in Cream

Bread-and-Butter Pudding

FOR TED AND ME, breakfast has always been grabbed on the run. I have my juice, fruit, and daily dose of vitamins. Ted has his coffee with bagels or coffee cake or the like. Before we were innkeepers, this was our routine six days a week.

But not on Sundays. Sunday was the day to sleep a little later (till 7:00 A.M.), go for a long run, and then come home to a huge breakfast. I would always bake bread on Saturdays, so breakfast on Sunday would consist of a loaf of homemade bread, omelettes, fresh fruit, and coffee for Ted. We loved to relax this way, enjoying every morsel. When we decided to become innkeepers, I knew I wanted to serve multi-course breakfasts, including juice, bread, fruit, and an entrée.

To me, winter means eating heartier foods, at breakfast as well as dinner. Our hearty breakfast entrées include scrambled eggs with caviar on puff pastry, cheese soufflés, baked apple pancakes, and, as in this menu, Bread-and-Butter Pudding. We began serving Bread-and-Butter Pudding the first year we owned the inn. Although it is normally a dessert, it makes a perfect breakfast dish. (When I first served it to our guests, I would make a lot of extra, so I could have it myself for breakfast *and* lunch.)

Our winter breakfast cakes are a bit more substantial than

the summer ones we make with fresh berries. Some of our favorite winter cakes are warm gingerbread, pumpkin and cranberry cake, and squash and pecan cake. Carrot cake, as in this menu, is the old standby. It seems that our guests never tire of a good carrot cake, and they like this one.

The fruit dishes we serve in the winter—such as grilled grapefruit, baked bananas, and apricot and prune compote—are mostly warm. Good old Bananas in Cream is an exception. This hearty dish is both the easiest and the most popular of our fruit courses, and it knows no seasons.

Pick a nice snowy morning, add a fire in the fireplace, make a batch of Bread-and-Butter Pudding, and feel the warmth.

Carrot Cake

Carrot cakes never seem to go out of style. We like to serve this for breakfast slightly warmed, with confectioner's sugar dusted on top. If you make this for dessert, add a cream cheese frosting.

1 cup chopped walnuts
3 cups sifted all-purpose
  flour
2 cups sugar
2 teaspoons ground
  cinnamon
1½ teaspoons baking soda
1 teaspoon baking powder
½ teaspoon salt

1 8½-ounce can crushed
  pineapple, drained, syrup
  reserved
3 eggs, lightly beaten
1½ cups corn oil
2 teaspoons vanilla extract
½ cup shredded coconut
2½ cups finely shredded
  carrots

Preheat the oven to 325°. Place the walnuts in a single layer on a baking sheet. Toast the nuts 10 minutes, or until they turn golden brown. Set them aside to cool.

Grease and lightly flour a Bundt pan.

Mix together the flour, sugar, cinnamon, baking soda, baking powder, and salt. Add the pineapple syrup, eggs, corn oil, and vanilla extract, and beat well. Fold in the pineapple, toasted walnuts, coconut, and shredded carrots.

Pour the batter into the greased Bundt pan. Bake the cake 1 hour and 15 minutes, or until a cake tester inserted in the center comes out clean.

Place the pan on a wire rack to cool for 10 minutes. Loosen the edges of the cake, then turn it out on a wire rack, and let it cool completely.

Sift confectioner's sugar over the cake before cutting it.

Serves 12

Bananas in Cream

For this dish, we always toast the almonds, and serve them still warm from the oven. The combination of cold cream and warm nuts is an unexpected delight.

2 ripe bananas   ¼ cup sliced almonds
¼ cup heavy cream

Preheat the oven to 350°. Place the almonds in a single layer on a baking sheet, and toast them 10 minutes.

Just before the nuts are ready, slice a banana diagonally into each of two bowls. Top each banana with 2 tablespoons heavy cream, and sprinkle each with 2 tablespoons warm toasted almonds.

Serve immediately.

Serves 2

Bread-and-Butter Pudding

I adore both bread and custards, so this combination is truly my favorite breakfast dish.

To make the pudding more festive, cook 1 cup fresh or frozen cranberries in 2 tablespoons orange juice just until the skins of the berries begin to pop. Sprinkle them over the bread before adding the custard.

1 1-pound loaf french bread, cut into 1½-inch rounds
6 tablespoons unsalted butter
3 eggs
4 egg yolks
½ cup sugar
Pinch salt
1½ cups milk
1 cup half-and-half
1 tablespoon vanilla extract

Butter one side of each round of french bread, and place the pieces buttered side up in a single layer in a large baking dish.

Preheat the oven to 375°. In a large bowl, thoroughly mix the eggs, egg yolks, sugar, and salt.

Scald the milk and half-and-half in a heavy-bottomed saucepan (heat them until tiny bubbles form around the edge of the pan). Remove the pan from the heat, and slowly add the milk and cream to the egg mixture, whisking briskly. Stir in the vanilla. Pour the milk-egg mixture over the bread in the baking dish (the bread will float to the top).

Place the filled baking dish in another baking dish large enough to hold it, and place the larger dish in the oven. Add enough boiling water to the larger dish to come halfway up the sides of the filled dish.

Bake for about 35 to 45 minutes, or until the custard is set.

Serve the pudding with confectioner's sugar sprinkled on top. It goes well with sautéed sliced ham.

Serves 5

LUNCHEON

A GALA LUNCHEON

Tomato Bisque

Scallops in Puff Pastry

Homemade Caramel Ice Cream in Lace Cups

WRITING DOWN THIS LUNCHEON MENU brings a smile to my face because of my wonderful, happy memories of serving these dishes.

The Scallops in Puff Pastry are one of our guests' favorite appetizers. This dish has helped establish our reputation.

In July 1988, the Arabian Peninsula Affairs Division of the Department of the Treasury used our inn as a meeting site. The group not only had our breakfasts and dinners while here, but we also prepared lunch for them daily. We found out that a couple of the people absolutely loved scallops, so I changed one of my menus and prepared this dish for their last luncheon here. The *oohs* and *aahs* that came from the dining room were well worth the effort.

A month later we received an unexpected gift. Beautifully framed was a handwritten thank-you on Treasury note paper and a dollar bill signed by the Secretary of the Treasury, James Baker, and the Treasurer of the United States. Accompanying the gift was a typed letter of gratitude from Charles Schotta, the Deputy Assistant Secretary. We had the letter framed to match the memento, and now both hang just outside the dining room entrance.

In his letter Charles Schotta wrote, "Chris, we can't say

enough good things about your splendid cuisine—the 'Coquilles St. Jacques en Feuilleté Chris' were simply superb!"

The scallops were the first course we served the food critic from the *Portland Sunday Telegram*, who said that the "tender . . . scallops in a delicate *beurre blanc* with a fine julienne of carrot and leeks, arranged with strips of buttery . . . puff pastry, were delicious." She gave us four stars.

The Homemade Caramel Ice Cream in Lace Cups is an all-time favorite. The first time I made the lace cups was for Thanksgiving one year. As I got started I was thinking of having myself committed to a mental hospital for adding something so difficult to an already herculean menu. But, as I learned, making the cups isn't so difficult after all, and, second, what a spectacular presentation they make! I make the cookies extra large so they look like wide petals of flowers that have just blossomed.

This is a special and exciting luncheon to be enjoyed any time of the year.

Tomato Bisque

For most people tomato bisque is a familiar and comforting dish, which is probably why this is one of our more popular soups. Because we use canned tomatoes, this soup can be made year round. We serve it as part of our Thanksgiving dinner.

½ cup (¼ pound) unsalted butter
2 garlic cloves, minced
½ cup chopped onion
2 leeks, white part only, chopped
3 tablespoons all-purpose flour
4 cups chicken stock
1 32-ounce can crushed Italian plum tomatoes

¼ cup chopped fresh parsley
2 tablespoons chopped fresh basil (or 1 teaspoon dried basil)
¼ cup dry white wine
1 cup heavy cream
Fresh-ground black pepper to taste
Sour cream

In a large kettle, melt the butter. Add the garlic, onion, and leeks, and sauté them until soft, about 5 minutes. Add the flour, and stir for 3 minutes. Gradually whisk in the chicken stock, and then the tomatoes. Continue to whisk until the mixture comes to a boil. Reduce the heat, and simmer for 15 minutes.

Stir in the parsley, basil, white wine, and cream. Remove the kettle from the heat, and purée the mixture in a food processor or blender until it is smooth. Transfer the mixture back to the kettle.

Add the pepper. Reheat the soup, and serve each bowl with a dollop of sour cream.

Serves 8

Scallops in Puff Pastry

This is an elegant and impressive luncheon entrée. The vegetables and puff pastry can be cooked ahead for ease in preparation and serving. You can find puff pastry in the freezer section of the grocery store.

4 4-by-5-inch pieces frozen puff pastry, thawed
1 egg yolk
1 small onion, minced fine
2 leeks, white part only, cut into julienne strips
2 carrots, cut into julienne strips
1 red bell pepper, cut into julienne strips

¾ cup plus 3 tablespoons unsalted butter
Salt and fresh-ground black pepper to taste
½ cup dry vermouth
¼ cup fish stock
1 pound fresh scallops
½ cup heavy cream

Place the puff pastry pieces on a baking sheet. Combine the egg yolk with 2 teaspoons water, and brush the tops of the pastry pieces with some of the egg wash. Chill the pieces for 15 minutes.

Preheat the oven to 400°. Again brush the tops of the pastry pieces with the egg wash, and bake them for 15 minutes, or until they are golden brown. Transfer the pastries to a rack, and let them cool.

In a skillet, melt the 3 tablespoons unsalted butter. Add the onion, leeks, carrots, and red pepper, and sauté the vegetables until they are barely tender, about 3 minutes. Season them with salt and pepper. Keep them warm.

In a saucepan, combine the vermouth, the fish stock, and black pepper to taste. Bring the mixture to a boil. Add the scallops, and boil just until the scallops are opaque, not more than 2 minutes. Strain the mixture, reserving both the scallops and liquid.

Return the liquid to the saucepan. Over medium-high heat, reduce the liquid by one-half. Add the heavy cream, stir with a whisk, and cook until the sauce thickens, about 10 minutes.

Cut the remaining butter into small pieces. Whisk it into the sauce, one piece at a time.

Add the vegetables and scallops to the sauce, and stir until they are coated. Reduce the heat to low.

Preheat the oven to 400°. With a serrated knife, cut off the top third of each pastry to make a lid. Gently scoop out any uncooked dough with a fork. Place the pastries on a baking sheet, then heat them in the oven for 2 minutes.

Place the bottoms of the pastries on individual plates.

Spoon the scallop mixture over the pastries, and top the pastries with the lids.

Serves 4 for lunch or 6 as an appetizer

Homemade Caramel Ice Cream
in Lace Cups

We serve this dessert often, in both the summer and the winter. Its presentation is nothing short of pure drama.

FOR THE LACE CUPS:

½ cup ground toasted walnuts (to toast walnuts, see page 39)
⅓ cup firmly packed dark brown sugar
4 tablespoons unsalted butter

¼ cup light corn syrup
½ teaspoon finely chopped lemon zest
½ cup all-purpose flour

FOR THE ICE CREAM:

2¾ cups heavy cream
1½ cups sugar
8 egg yolks

2 cups milk
½ vanilla bean, halved lengthwise

Make the lace cups: Generously grease three large baking sheets. Preheat the oven to 325°.

In a medium saucepan, combine the brown sugar, butter, corn syrup, and lemon zest. Cook over low heat until the butter is melted and the sugar is dissolved. Add the flour and nuts, and stir until the mixture is well blended.

Pour three circles of batter onto each of two baking sheets, and two circles onto the third baking sheet. Spread the circles with the bottom of a large spoon, allowing plenty of space between them. Bake one sheet of cookies until the cookies are lightly browned, approximately 13 minutes. Let them cool for 1 minute.

Using a large spatula, carefully remove one cookie. Mold it around the sides of an inverted custard cup, pinching the sides to form pleats. Repeat with the remaining cookies. Let the cookies cool for 15 minutes.

Gently remove the cookies from the custard cups, and place them right side up on a wire rack.

Make the caramel ice cream: In a medium saucepan over

medium heat, bring ¾ cup of heavy cream just to a simmer; do not let it boil.

In a heavy, medium saucepan, stir 1 cup of the sugar over high heat with a wooden spoon until the sugar melts and turns medium brown, about 5 minutes. Take the pan off the heat, and slowly stir the warm cream into the caramel, taking care that the mixture does not splatter. Cook the caramel sauce over low heat, stirring constantly with a wire whisk, until the caramel is completely melted, 1 to 2 minutes. Remove the pan from the heat.

In a small bowl, whisk the egg yolks and remaining sugar together until they are well blended.

In a saucepan, bring the remaining heavy cream, milk, and vanilla bean just to a boil. Pour the hot cream mixture into the egg-yolk mixture in a thin stream, whisking constantly. Return the mixture to the saucepan, and cook it over moderately low heat, stirring constantly, until the custard thickens enough to lightly coat the back of a spoon, 5 to 7 minutes. Do not let the mixture come to a boil. Remove it from the heat, and stir the caramel sauce into it.

Remove the vanilla bean, and scrape the seeds back into the mixture. Pour the mixture into a stainless steel bowl. Set the bowl in a basin of ice and water, and let it stand, stirring occasionally, until the mixture has cooled to room temperature. Cover and refrigerate it for at least four hours, or until it is very cold.

Pour the custard into an ice cream maker, and freeze according to the manufacturer's instructions.

Spoon the ice cream into the lace cups, and serve immediately.

Serves 8

TEA

NEW YEAR'S TEA

Wild Mushroom Tartlets

Pear and Prosciutto Cornets with Ginger Cream

Shortbread with Poppyseeds

Heart-shaped Toasts with Red and Black Caviars

Beggar's Purses with Lobster Filling

Chocolate Chestnut Torte

Hazelnut Sables

Fruit Tartlets

WE HAD OUR FIRST New Year's Eve celebration at the inn in 1988, and we have continued the tradition each year since. The event always centers on glorious food. It's a very special way of celebrating the new year with old and new friends. Our New Year's celebrations have brought us Tom Hoffmann, a local guitarist and composer, who plays wonderful classical guitar music during the entire evening. Guests Lee and Carol Hall and Chick and Madine Parakilas have always come, too— they are part of the tradition.

New Year's Eve is the night we pull out all the stops for dinner. On this evening we begin cocktail hour at 7:30, and do not seat our guests for dinner until 8:30. We experiment with new foods; I always seem determined to wear myself out on this day by making the most complicated meal I can imagine. The year I made the individual cranberry chocolate cakes I did not plan on five hours just to assemble them, so you can imagine what the rest of the day was like. I think that was the year Ted posted a sign on the kitchen door that read, "Don't Even Think of Entering If You Want Dinner Tonight."

After dinner we bring out the hats, noisemakers, and champagne. We have a toast at midnight and sing "Auld Lang Syne" to welcome in the New Year.

We are very happy, however, that some events that have occurred during our New Year's celebrations have *not* become tradition. New Year's Eve of 1989 is one day that we will never forget. After breakfast on the thirty-first, the guest room directly above the living room developed a leak in the bathroom. Soon we had a bucket on the floor in the middle of the living room. Before I could have a nervous breakdown, Ted managed to have the leak fixed. But it was raining that day, and in the middle of the afternoon the roof started leaking. We had leaks in three guest rooms, on our porch, and in the carriage house hallway. We figured out that we had ice jams on the back side of the inn. There was only one thing to do: Ted got out his chain saw and started tearing out all the wooden gutters on the back side of the inn. It was a sight that none of us will forget—Ted hanging off the side of the building in the freezing rain. It has been said that these things always happen when you have a full house, and we did.

For Ted and me, New Year's Eve is always the hardest and longest day of the year—but also the most gratifying.

In 1990 we decided to begin our New Year's festivities with a high tea on Sunday, December 30, at 3:00, instead of serving dinner that night. We had never had a high tea at the inn before, and we thought this would be a great time to try it. The tea was an overwhelming success. For me it was wonderful to sit down with the guests, relax, and enjoy the entire evening, because the work had already been done. We just sat around the fireplace, drank Earl Grey and herbal lemon teas, ate glorious little foods, had wonderful conversations, renewed old friendships, and made new ones.

Gail Greco asked if she could feature our New Year's tea in her upcoming book, *Teatime at the Inn*. On December 27 we prepared most of the food, set up the formal living room for tea in front of the fireplace, poured champagne, set out hats and noisemakers, graced the tables with the antique linens my grandmother had made, blew up balloons, sprinkled golden confetti and strewed golden streamers, and spent the day being photographed for the book.

The recipes here are those we included in *Teatime at the Inn* and served for our first New Year's tea. We hope high tea will always be part of our New Year's tradition, and we hope it will become a part of yours.

WILD MUSHROOM TARTLETS

The tartlet shells can be made ahead and frozen.

FOR THE TARTLET SHELLS:
2 cups flour
Pinch salt
½ teaspoon sugar

¾ cup (⅜ pound) unsalted
    butter, cut into small
    pieces and chilled

FOR THE FILLING:
1 ounce dried porcini
    mushrooms
1 leek, sliced thin
3 tablespoons unsalted
    butter
1 pound small mushrooms,
    chopped fine
2 tablespoons flour

3 tablespoons Madeira wine
½ cup *crème fraîche* (see
    page 31)
Salt and fresh-ground pepper
    to taste
¼ cup minced parsley

Make the shells: Stir together the flour, salt, and sugar. Cut in the butter until the mixture resembles cornmeal. Slowly blend in 3 tablespoons ice water. The pastry will pull away from the sides of the bowl.

Remove the pastry from the bowl. On a floured surface, shape it into a ball, and wrap it in plastic. Refrigerate it for 30 minutes.

Preheat the oven to 425°.

Roll out the pastry, cut it into 3-inch rounds, and use it to line individual tartlet pans. Prick the dough lightly with a fork. Place the shells on a baking sheet, line them with foil, and fill them with rice or pie weights. Place the baking sheet in the oven, and bake the shells 10 minutes. Carefully remove the foil and rice, and bake the shells another 5 to 10 minutes, or until they are golden brown. Cool the tartlets in their pans on a rack, then remove the shells carefully from the pans.

Make the filling: Soak the porcini in hot water to cover for 30 minutes. Drain well, reserving the liquid for another use. Chop the porcini fine.

Preheat the oven to 375°.

In a large skillet, melt the butter. Cook the leeks in the

melted butter over low heat, covered, for 10 minutes. Add the porcini and other mushrooms and cook, stirring, until the liquid from the mushrooms is evaporated. Stir in the flour, and cook for 2 minutes. Stir in the Madeira, *crème fraîche*, and salt and pepper, and cook the filling, stirring, for 5 minutes. Remove the skillet from the heat, and stir in the minced parsley. Let the filling cool.

Place the tartlet shells on a baking sheet. Divide the filling among the tartlet shells, smoothing the tops. Bake the tartlets 10 minutes. Serve them warm.

Makes 40 tartlets

Prosciutto and Pear Cornets
with Ginger Cream

Mascarpone is a creamy Italian cheese found in some specialty stores. If you can't find it, substitute 3 ounces softened cream cheese and 2 tablespoons heavy cream.

4 ounces mascarpone cheese
1 teaspoon grated fresh
   ginger
1 teaspoon coarse-grain
   mustard

4 firm pears
Juice of 2 lemons
¼ pound prosciutto, sliced
   paper-thin, slices halved

Beat together the mascarpone cheese, ginger, and mustard until the mixture smooth.

Halve and core the pears, then cut each half lengthwise into eight pieces. In a bowl, toss the pears gently with the lemon juice to coat them. Cover the broader end of each pear slice with approximately ½ teaspoon of filling. Center the pear on one slice of prosciutto and wrap the pear in it, making a horn shape.

Makes 32 cornets

Shortbread with Poppyseeds

This shortbread is great to have on hand. It goes as well with a glass of lemonade as with a cup of tea.

¾ cup (⅜ pound) unsalted butter, at room temperature

½ cup sugar
2 cups flour
¼ cup poppyseeds

Grease well a shortbread mold. Preheat the oven to 375°.

Cream the butter until it is light colored and fluffy. Gradually beat in the sugar, and continue beating until the mixture is soft and light. On low speed, mix in the flour and poppyseeds. Mix just until the dough is blended (it will be crumbly).

Press the dough into the mold. Bake the shortbread until it is golden brown, approximately 15 to 20 minutes. Cool it on a rack before unmolding it.

The shortbread will keep for a week in an airtight container.

Heart-Shaped Toasts
with Red and Black Caviars

If you like, you can serve these hearts with bowls of sieved hard-boiled egg yolks, or fine-grated onions, or whipped *crème fraîche*. For our tea, I prefer to serve the hearts plain.

Thin-sliced white bread,
  preferably homemade
Unsalted butter, at room
  temperature

Red salmon roe caviar
Black caviar

Remove the crusts from the bread, and, using a heart-shaped cutter, cut out hearts.

Preheat the broiler. Place the hearts on a baking sheet, and place the baking sheet under the broiler. Lightly toast the hearts on both sides. Let them cool on a wire rack.

Just before serving, spread each heart with a thin layer of unsalted butter. Spread one half of the heart with red caviar and the other half with black caviar. Serve immediately.

Beggars' Purses with Lobster Filling

Because of their shape and filling (and despite their name), these "purses" are an elegant treat. We serve them during our 6:00 to 7:00 P.M. cocktail reception as well as for high tea.

5 shallots, chopped fine
1¼ cups unsalted butter
1 cup cooked lobster meat, chopped
Juice of 1 lemon

1 pound frozen phyllo dough (available in the freezer section of most supermarkets), thawed
Salt and pepper to taste

In a small pan, melt ¼ cup butter. Sauté the shallots until they are soft, about 3 minutes. Let them cool.

In a bowl, combine the lobster meat, shallots, lemon juice, salt, and pepper.

Preheat the oven to 350°.

In a saucepan, melt the remaining 1 cup butter. Lay one phyllo sheet on a work surface, and brush it lightly with the butter. Top with two more phyllo sheets, buttering each as you layer them. Cut the stacked, buttered phyllo into 4-inch squares. Place 1 teaspoon of the lobster filling in the center of each square. Gather the corners together over the center, and crimp firmly to form purses. Transfer the purses to baking sheets, spacing them 1 inch apart. Lightly brush the tops of the purses with melted butter.

Bake the purses until they are crisp and golden brown, approximately 20 minutes. Serve them hot.

Makes 50 Beggars' Purses

Chocolate Chestnut Torte

Perfect for the holidays, this rich dessert is a hit at our Christmas parties as well as at New Year's tea.

FOR THE TORTE:

1 pound vacuum-packed whole chestnuts
⅓ cup heavy cream
½ cup (¼ pound) unsalted butter, at room temperature

¾ cup sugar
10 ounces semisweet chocolate, chopped and melted
6 large eggs, separated
Pinch salt

FOR THE GLAZE:

6 ounces semisweet chocolate, chopped fine

½ cup heavy cream

Make the torte: Grease a 9-inch springform pan, and line the bottom with parchment paper. Grease the paper, and dust the bottom and side of the pan with flour.

In a food processor, purée the chestnuts until they are smooth, adding 1 tablespoon of water if necessary. Transfer the purée to a large bowl, and add the cream. Whisk together the purée and the cream until the mixture is smooth. Whisk in the butter and sugar. Stir in the chocolate. Whisk in the egg yolks one at a time, beating well after each addition.

Preheat the oven to 350°.

Beat the egg whites with a pinch of salt until the meringue holds stiff peaks. Lightly stir about one-third of the meringue into the chocolate mixture to lighten it, and then gently fold in the remaining meringue. Pour the batter into the prepared pan, smooth the top, and bake the torte 45 to 55 minutes, until the top is cracked.

Cool the torte in its pan on a wire rack for 15 minutes. Remove the side of the pan. Invert the torte onto a serving platter, and remove the bottom of the pan. Let the torte cool completely.

Make the glaze: Put the chocolate in a small bowl. In a saucepan, bring the cream to a boil. Pour the cream over the chocolate. Stir the mixture until the chocolate is melted and the glaze is smooth. Spread the glaze evenly over the top and sides of the torte.

This torte should be served the same day it is made.

Serves 8

Hazelnut Sables

These cookies will keep about one week in an airtight container.

¾ cup whole hazelnuts
⅔ cup plus 2 tablespoons confectioner's sugar
¾ cup (⅜ pound) unsalted butter, at room temperature

½ teaspoon vanilla extract
2 egg yolks
Pinch salt
2 cups all-purpose flour
1 egg white

Preheat the oven to 350°. Spread the hazelnuts in a single layer on a baking sheet, and toast them 15 minutes. While the nuts are still warm, rub them in a towel, a few at a time, to remove their skins. Let the nuts cool.

In a food processor, grind fine ½ cup of the hazelnuts with 2 tablespoons confectioner's sugar. Set the mixture aside.

Cream the butter with the remaining confectioner's sugar until the mixture is light and fluffy. Add the vanilla extract, egg yolks, and salt, and beat until the ingredients are combined. Beat in the hazelnut mixture. Beat in the flour, and continue beating until the dough is well combined. Wrap the dough in plastic, and chill it at least 6 hours or overnight.

Work with just one-fourth of the dough at a time, keeping the remaining dough in the refrigerator. Roll the dough out ¼-inch thick. Cut it into shapes with cookie cutters, and immediately transfer the cookies to buttered baking sheets. Chill the cookies on the sheets for 30 minutes.

Preheat the oven to 350°. Chop the remaining ¼ cup hazelnuts fine.

In a small bowl, beat the egg white together with 1 teaspoon water. Brush the cookies lightly with the egg wash and sprinkle them with the chopped hazelnuts. Bake the cookies for 15 to 20 minutes, or until they are pale golden. Remove them to a rack to cool.

Store the sables in an airtight container.

Makes about 48 cookies

Fruit Tartlets

For our New Year's tea I use clementines, kiwi fruit, and strawberries in these tartlets. The pastry cream can be made one day ahead and stored in a covered container in the refrigerator.

About 40 tartlet shells (see page 58)
1 cup milk
3 egg yolks
⅓ cup sugar
2 tablespoons flour
½ teaspoon vanilla extract
About 1 tablespoon butter
Assorted fresh fruits
¾ cup jelly, marmalade, or preserves, or a combination of these

Make the pastry cream: Pour the milk into a saucepan, and bring it to a boil. Remove the pan from the heat.

In a bowl, beat the sugar and egg yolks together with a wire whisk, until the mixture whitens. Gently whisk in the flour. Pour the hot milk into the egg and sugar mixture, whisking continuously. Pour the mixture back into the saucepan, and bring it to a boil, stirring constantly with the whisk. Boil the mixture for 1 minute, stirring. Pour the mixture into a bowl, stir in the vanilla, and rub the surface of the cream with butter to keep a skin from forming as the mixture cools.

Spread 1 tablespoon pastry cream in each tartlet shell. Decoratively arrange the fruit on top of the pastry cream. For a strawberry tartlet, use one whole strawberry. For a kiwi tartlet, slice the kiwi, and arrange three to four slices, overlapping, in a ring. For a clementine tartlet, use three to five segments, depending on the size of the tartlet shell.

Glaze the shells: For the strawberry tartlets, use red currant jelly; for the clementine tartlets, use orange marmalade; and for the kiwi fruit, use apricot preserves. Melt each quarter cup of jelly, marmalade, or preserves with 1 teaspoon water. Strain the marmalade or preserves. Brush the tops of the fruits with the glaze.

Serve the tartlets immediately.

Makes 40 tartlets

DINNER

SPRING DINNER

Asparagus with Prosciutto and Mustard Vinaigrette

Spinach Soup

Rack of Lamb with Chive Sauce

New Potatoes with Parsley

Individual Strawberry Charlottes

THERE IS SOMETHING REJUVENATING in hearing the birds sing-
ing for the first time in the spring, or in seeing the first trees
bud out, the tulips and daffodils rise up and flower, the for-
sythia bloom in all its golden glory, or the grass turn from
brown to green. These are all wonderful signs that spring is
upon us; everything seems fresh and new. Up here in Maine
spring arrives later than in most of the country, and sometimes
we feel as though we are transported from winter to summer
in a matter of days.

Soon it is late spring, and the lupines bloom. The fields of
pink, purple, and white lupines are among the most incredible
of sights.

At our inn, spring means sprucing up in preparation for the
busy summer months ahead. The paint and paintbrushes come
out, the gardens and lawn are raked, the walks are swept, and
all the windows are washed. This is the time to clean up from
the effects of winter.

The foods of spring are every bit as exciting as the season's
sights, sounds, and activities. This is the time of year for my

two favorite vegetables, asparagus and beet greens. They are real spring tonics.

I love asparagus in any form—raw, blanched and served cold in a salad or alone with a vinaigrette, or warm with melted butter. Because Ted's dad raised asparagus, when we were first married we would visit him during asparagus season and bring home about 15 pounds. We would eat asparagus every day of the week. It was at Ted's parents' that I first had steamed asparagus on toast with melted butter—perhaps the best lunch ever. When we planned our own garden a couple of years later, asparagus beds were high priority.

Even our dog loves asparagus. As soon as Destiny hears me breaking off the tough ends, even if she seems to be in deep sleep, she will sit right at attention by the kitchen door and just wait for me to feed her raw asparagus.

Beet greens, simply sautéed in a little olive oil and butter, are heavenly. Most of our guests have never had tender young beet greens; they have always thrown away the tops of the beets they buy (as they should, because most are tough). But the greens that come before the beets develop, or those with little beets attached, can be a treat. If you can find early beet greens, try them. You will not be disappointed.

Asparagus with Prosciutto and Mustard Vinaigrette

To trim the ends of asparagus, just hold a spear at both ends and bend it gently; it will break at just the right spot. If you cut off the end with a knife, you cannot tell exactly where the tough part begins.

2 garlic cloves, crushed
2 egg yolks, at room
   temperature
½ teaspoon dry mustard
2 tablespoons Dijon mustard
¼ cup red wine vinegar
1 tablespoon fresh lemon
   juice

¾ cup olive oil
Salt
Fresh-ground pepper to taste
1 pound fresh asparagus,
   ends trimmed
6 ounces prosciutto, sliced
   thin

Combine the garlic, egg yolks, mustards, vinegar, and lemon juice in a food processor or blender. With the machine running, very slowly add the olive oil in a thin stream. Season with salt and pepper. Set the vinaigrette aside.

In a large kettle, bring to a rapid boil 4 quarts salted water. Blanch the asparagus for 5 minutes. Remove the kettle from the heat. With tongs, carefully remove the asparagus and plunge it into ice water to stop the cooking process. When the asparagus is cold, lift it from the water, and dry it completely on paper towels.

Make a little pool of the mustard vinaigrette in the middle of each plate. Wrap the base of each asparagus spear with prosciutto, and arrange the spears in the center of the plates, aligning the tips.

Refrigerate the remaining vinaigrette, and use it later as salad dressing.

Serves 4

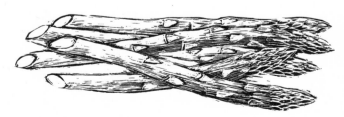

Spinach Soup

Chopping the spinach rather than puréeing it gives this soup an interesting texture. Try to use just-picked young and tender spinach leaves for the most wonderful results.

4 pounds fresh spinach,
  blanched
6 tablespoons unsalted
  butter
1 cup chopped onion
½ cup chopped leeks, white
  part only

1 garlic clove, minced
7 cups chicken stock
¼ cup uncooked white rice
¼ teaspoon ground nutmeg
Salt and fresh-ground pepper
  to taste
Sour cream

Chop the spinach coarsely.

In a kettle, melt 2 tablespoons of the unsalted butter. Add the onion, leeks, and garlic, and sauté them until they are translucent, approximately 5 minutes. Add the remaining butter, and when it is melted add the spinach. Sauté the spinach and onion mixture for an additional 5 minutes. Add the chicken stock to the kettle. Bring the stock to a boil, add the rice, and simmer for 20 minutes. Add the nutmeg, salt, and pepper, and serve the soup, garnished with sour cream.

Serves 6

Rack of Lamb with Chive Sauce

Rack of lamb is probably the most elegant, the most well-loved, and the easiest to prepare of all entrées that we serve at the inn. We have been serving it with this chive sauce since we first started serving dinners.

2 racks of lamb, trimmed
3 tablespoons olive oil
Salt and fresh-ground pepper
   to taste
2 tablespoons unsalted
   butter
1 leek, white part only,
   chopped fine
1 large bunch chives,
   coarsely chopped

¼ cup white wine
¼ cup beef stock
¼ cup chicken stock
½ cup *crème fraîche* (see
   page 31), at room
   temperature
Additional chopped chives

Place the lamb racks in a roasting pan. Rub all sides of the lamb with the olive oil. Sprinkle generously with salt and pepper. Cover the lamb, and refrigerate it for 6 hours.

Preheat the oven to 350°. Place the roasting pan on the stove top over high heat, and brown the lamb on all sides. Transfer the pan to the oven, and roast 25 minutes (for medium-rare lamb). Remove the lamb from the oven, cover it with foil, and allow it to rest for 10 minutes.

While the lamb is roasting, prepare the sauce. In a small saucepan, melt the butter over low heat. Add the leek, and sauté until it is softened but not browned, approximately 5 minutes. Add most of the chives (reserve some for sprinkling over the chops), and stir over the heat for 1 minute. Add the white wine, and boil until it is slightly reduced. Add both the stocks, and boil until the liquid is reduced by half. Transfer the mixture to a food processor or blender, and purée it. Return the mixture to the saucepan.

In a small bowl, stir the *crème fraîche* until it is smooth and slightly runny. Add the *crème fraîche*, salt, and pepper to the saucepan, and stir over low heat until the sauce is warmed through, approximately 5 minutes. Keep the sauce warm.

Carve the lamb into chops. Spoon the sauce onto plates. Top with the lamb chops, and sprinkle the chops with the remaining chopped chives.

Serves 4

New Potatoes with Parsley

I love the first potatoes of the season. I always boil extra, to sauté for breakfast. I slice an onion and sauté it in butter until it is lightly browned. I add the potato slices and continue to sauté, adding plenty of fresh-ground black pepper, and a pinch of salt. The leftovers are sometimes even better than the original!

1 pound small new red
  potatoes, unpeeled
Salt to taste
2 tablespoons unsalted
  butter

¼ cup finely chopped Italian
  parsley
Fresh-ground pepper to taste

Rinse the potatoes, drain them, and put them in a saucepan. Cover them with water, and salt to taste. Bring the water to a boil, and simmer the potatoes 15 to 20 minutes, or until they are tender.

Drain the potatoes, and return them to the saucepan. Add the butter, and roll the potatoes in it. Add the chopped parsley and pepper, and continue to roll the potatoes around until they are well coated. Serve.

Serves 4

Individual Strawberry Charlottes

For the best taste, be sure your strawberries are fully ripe. This dessert is made using the French bavarian cream method. If you have time to make your own ladyfingers, the result is worth the effort.

1 quart strawberries, hulled
1¼ cups confectioner's
  sugar, sifted
2 envelopes unflavored
  gelatin

2 cups heavy cream
2 tablespoons kirsch
18 ladyfingers, halved
Whipped cream

FOR THE STRAWBERRY SAUCE:
1 pint strawberries, hulled
⅓ cup sugar

2 tablespoons kirsch

In a food processor or blender, purée the 1 quart strawberries. Pour the purée into a bowl, and whisk in the confectioner's sugar. Set the bowl over a pan of simmering water (so the water does not touch the bowl), and sprinkle the gelatin over the purée. Stir while the purée warms and the gelatin dissolves. When the gelatin has dissolved, remove the bowl from the heat. Cover the bowl, and refrigerate the purée until it is cold.

Whip the 2 cups heavy cream until soft peaks form. Fold the cream and 2 tablespoons of the kirsch into the chilled purée. Cover the bowl, and refrigerate it.

Line the bottom and sides of six large balloon-style wine glasses with the ladyfingers, rounded sides out. Spoon the strawberry mixture into the glasses, smoothing the tops. Refrigerate the glasses for 4 hours.

Make the strawberry sauce: Place one cup strawberries and the ⅓ cup sugar in the bowl of a food processor, and purée until smooth. Add the 2 tablespoons kirsch.

Slice the other cup of strawberries, and arrange the slices in concentric circles covering the surface of each charlotte. Pipe cream decoratively into the center of each.

Serve the charlottes with the strawberry sauce on the side.

Serves 6

SUMMER DINNER

Risotto Primavera

Cold Cream of Vidalia Onion Soup

Grilled Swordfish with Horseradish Butter

Blueberry-Raspberry Pie

As you might expect, the summer months are the busiest for us. This is the time when we see the greatest number of guests and when we truly work the hardest. These are the months when our produce is at its peak, when the fruit is just wonderful. The sights and smells in the kitchen are sometimes breathtaking. I can't wait for our deliveries from Bambi and Jan twice a week. The first batch of young green beans makes me smile from ear to ear, and the green peas are worth the effort of shelling them. I get excited when I see that first tray of freshly picked raspberries (I won't say how many I can eat at one time), the fennel for roasting, the most beautiful of lettuces, the reddest of tomatoes, the wonderful little yellow pear tomatoes, and the corn for soufflés—the list could go on and on. I am truly like a child in a candy store.

We are also like squirrels getting ready for winter. We bake a lot of blueberry lemon cakes and raspberry streusel cakes for the freezer; we freeze blueberries; we make soups for the freezer as well as for dinner. We prepare foods for freezing as soon as they are picked to retain optimum freshness and taste. When we serve our Asparagus and Pea Soup or our Sorrel Soup in February, you might truly think that the asparagus or sorrel had been picked just that morning. When we make our corn soufflé in December, you might imagine the corn kernels were just scraped off the cob. Amazingly, all of this work is being accomplished while we are serving dinner each night of the week.

The grounds of the inn are beautiful this time of year, with the flowers in full bloom. It is wonderful to see guests relaxing in the lawn chairs, or in the hammock in a peaceful spot overlooking the river. Our canoe sits waiting for us. We dream of owning a sailboat, too. . . . Well, some day.

Risotto Primavera

I am a big risotto fan and this is my favorite. Although risotto is not at its best the day after it is made, I still save the leftovers for my lunch.

I know *primavera* means spring, but most of the vegetables for this risotto are available in the summer months. Try other vegetables, too; there is no limit to the kinds that you can use.

The hardest part of this dish is that it takes approximately 35 minutes of constant stirring. Once you taste it, though, you will agree that the result is very much worth the effort.

¼ cup olive oil
1 large onion, chopped fine
1 garlic clove, minced
1 pound Arborio rice (available in Italian groceries and other specialty stores)
½ cup dry white wine
6 cups chicken stock
¼ pound mushrooms, sliced thin
1 large red bell pepper, cut in 1-inch squares

¼ pound snow peas (cut in half diagonally)
8 asparagus spears (cut in diagonal 1-inch pieces)
4 plum tomatoes, peeled, seeded, and chopped
¼ cup finely chopped Italian parsley
Salt and fresh-ground pepper to taste
½ cup grated Parmesan cheese

Heat the oil in a large skillet. Add the onion and garlic. Cook them over moderate heat, stirring until the onion is soft. Add the rice, and stir to coat it with the oil. Add the wine, and stir until it is absorbed.

Meanwhile, bring the chicken stock to a boil, lower the heat, and keep the stock at a simmer.

Begin adding the stock to the rice, one-half cup at a time. Stir until each addition is absorbed.

After 4 cups of the stock have been absorbed, add, in the following order, the mushrooms, red bell pepper, snow peas, asparagus, and tomatoes; stir well constantly. Add more stock as needed. When all the liquid is absorbed, add the parsley, salt, and pepper.

Remove the skillet from the heat. Stir in the Parmesan cheese, and serve the risotto at once.

Serves 8

Cold Cream of Vidalia Onion Soup

Last year I discovered Vidalia onions (from Vidalia, Georgia),
and we have fallen in love with them. You can substitute
Spanish onions, but try to find the Vidalia when they are in
season. *Gourmet* magazine requested this recipe in the summer of 1991.

5 slices bacon, cut crosswise
into ½-inch strips
½ cup (¼ pound) unsalted
butter
3 pounds Vidalia onions,
sliced thin
6 garlic cloves
4 cups chicken stock
2 cups dry white wine
1 teaspoon crumbled dried
thyme leaves

2 cups *crème fraîche* (see
page 31)
2 tablespoons fresh lemon
juice
1 teaspoon ground white
pepper
1 teaspoon Dijon mustard
¼ teaspoon ground nutmeg
1 cup thinly sliced scallion

In a large kettle, cook the bacon until it is crisp, stirring
occasionally. Transfer it with a slotted spoon to paper towels
to drain.

Add the butter to the bacon fat in the kettle. When the
butter has melted, add the onions and garlic. Cover the kettle,
and cook the onions and garlic over low heat for 30 minutes,
stirring occasionally.

Add the chicken stock, wine, and thyme, and simmer the
mixture, covered, for 25 minutes.

In a food processor or blender, purée the mixture in batches.
Refrigerate the mixture, covered, until it is cold.

In a small bowl, stir the *crème fraîche* until it is smooth
and slightly runny. Whisk it, with the lemon juice, white
pepper, mustard, and nutmeg, into the chilled onion mixture.
Serve the soup in chilled bowls, sprinkled with the reserved
bacon and the sliced scallions.

Serves 10

Grilled Swordfish with Horseradish Butter

Be sure that your swordfish is absolutely fresh. We are fortunate to have a local fishing industry, and therefore access to the freshest fish. Our fishmonger knows that since all our guests eat the same entrée, if we receive a fish that is not fresh we have nothing to serve for dinner! When guests tell us that the fish we have served them is the best fish they have eaten, we tell them the main reason is the freshness. And we pass the compliment on to our fishmonger.

⅓ cup dry white wine
1 teaspoon grated lemon zest
Juice of 2 lemons
2 garlic cloves, minced

2 teaspoons Dijon mustard
½ cup olive oil
8 swordfish steaks (at least 1 inch thick)

FOR THE HORSERADISH BUTTER:

1 cup (½ pound) unsalted butter, at room temperature
1 tablespoon coarse-grain mustard
1 tablespoon prepared horseradish

3 garlic cloves, minced
¼ teaspoon Worcestershire sauce
Dash Tabasco sauce

In a bowl, whisk together the wine, lemon zest and juice, garlic, mustard, and olive oil.

Place the fish in a shallow, nonreactive baking dish. Pour the marinade over the fish. Pierce each steak with a fork, then turn the steak and pierce the other side. Marinate the fish in the refrigerator, covered, for 4 hours, turning the steak after 2 hours.

Meanwhile, make the horseradish butter: With an electric mixer, cream together the butter, mustard, horseradish, garlic, Worcestershire sauce, and Tabasco sauce until they are well blended. Refrigerate the butter until you are ready to use it.

Prepare a fire for grilling.

Grill the swordfish over hot coals for 5 to 6 minutes per side, brushing the fish often with the marinade.

Serve the swordfish immediately, topped with the horseradish butter.

Serves 8

Blueberry-Raspberry Pie

Blueberries are great, raspberries are the very best, and combined in this dessert they are unbeatable. There is no better way to celebrate summer than with the taste of fresh berries.

1 baked 9-inch pie shell
1 quart fresh blueberries
1 pint fresh raspberries

3 tablespoons cornstarch
¾ cup sugar
Whipped cream

Empty the blueberries into a strainer, and rinse them well. Drain them.

Blend the raspberries in a food processor. Pour them into a fine sieve, and press them to extract as much juice as possible. Discard the seeds. You should have at least 1 cup purée.

Pour 1 cup raspberry purée into a saucepan, and add the cornstarch, 1 cup of the blueberries, and the sugar.

Place the saucepan over moderate heat, and bring the berry mixture to a boil, stirring. When the mixture has thickened, add an additional 1 cup of the blueberries, and cook until the berries are heated through, about 5 minutes. Do not overcook the berries, or they will soften and lose their shape.

Spoon the mixture into the prepared pie shell. Smooth the top. Top with the remaining 2 cups blueberries.

Serve the pie at room temperature, garnished with whipped cream.

Serves 8

FALL DINNER

Baked Scallops

Cream of Pumpkin Soup

Roast Loin of Pork with Prunes, Apricots, and Madeira

Individual Apple Tarts with Maple Syrup
and Vanilla Ice Cream

FALL IS MY FAVORITE TIME of the year. Before we became innkeepers, Ted and I would go hiking in the White Mountains in New Hampshire every October. The scenery was beautiful, with clear blue skies, red and orange leaves on the trees and on the ground, and snow-capped Mount Washington in the background.

Now that we are innkeepers, we share our foliage season with guests from all over the world, many of whom have never seen leaves change their colors. We have no mountains here, but the combination of the blue sky, the blue water, and the colorful trees is spectacular. This is the time for long walks, on trails and on the beach.

Fall is also when we start eating heartier foods. The evenings are cool, and a bowl of hot soup just fills the need. Maine apples make delicious, filling desserts. From a nearby orchard, Clark's Cove Farm, we buy an assortment of apples—some to cook with, and some to leave out as snacks for our guests. We also serve the farm's unusual apple cider combinations, like MacRaz, MacIntosh apples with raspberries.

Because of the early frosts here, few green vegetables are left in autumn gardens, so now is the time to enjoy all those wonderful winter squashes and pumpkins. I love to decorate our inn with an assortment of unusual squashes and pumpkins. When Thanksgiving is upon us, we make squash and pumpkin pies and soups.

There is no place as special as New England in the fall.

Baked Scallops

Scallop harvesting in Maine begins in November. This is the time that in-shore scallops, also known as divers' scallops, are at their best. They are so sweet you can eat them raw. To ensure tender scallops, there are two important things to remember: Remove the gristle from the edge of the muscle, and keep the cooking time to a minimum.

1¼ cups fresh bread crumbs
3 garlic cloves, minced
3 tablespoons finely minced onion
¼ cup chopped parsley
¼ cup dry white wine
3 tablespoons lemon juice
Salt and fresh-ground pepper to taste

½ cup (¼ pound) unsalted butter, melted
2 tablespoons olive oil
1½ pounds scallops, gristle removed, patted dry
½ pound mushrooms, sliced thin

In a bowl, combine the bread crumbs, garlic, onion, parsley, white wine, lemon juice, and salt and pepper. Pour the melted butter over the mixture, and mix gently. Set the bowl aside.

Preheat the oven to 450°.

In a skillet, heat the olive oil. Add the scallops and mushrooms, and sauté them briefly. Drain them well. Season them with salt and pepper.

Grease well a shallow 2-quart baking dish. Fill the baking dish with the scallops and mushrooms. Spoon the bread-crumb mixture on top.

Place the dish in the oven, and bake for 8 minutes, or until the topping is golden brown. Serve immediately.

Serves 6

Cream of Pumpkin Soup

This soup really brings fall into our dining room. The toasted pumpkin seeds add a nice crunch. They are just as good to eat as a snack by themselves.

1 5-pound pumpkin, peeled and cubed (reserve the seeds)
1 medium russet potato, peeled and chopped
1 medium onion, chopped
7 cups chicken stock

2 tablespoons vegetable oil
Salt to taste
¼ teaspoon freshly grated nutmeg
⅛ teaspoon fresh-ground white pepper
2 cups light cream

Place the pumpkin, potato, and onion in a large kettle. Add the chicken stock. Place the pot over high heat, and bring the stock to a boil. Simmer, covered, for 1 hour, or until the pumpkin cubes are tender.

Meanwhile, toast the pumpkin seeds: Preheat the oven to 375°. Rinse the pumpkin seeds in cold water, and drain them in a colander. Pat them dry with paper towels, and put them in a bowl. Add the vegetable oil, and stir to coat the seeds well. Spread the seeds on a baking pan. Bake them 15 minutes, shaking the pan occasionally. Sprinkle the seeds with salt, and toss to mix well. Continue baking until the seeds are crisp and golden brown, approximately 5 minutes.

Remove the vegetables with a slotted spoon to a food processor. Purée the vegetables until smooth, in batches if necessary. Return the purée to the liquid in the kettle.

Add the salt, nutmeg, pepper, and cream to the pot. Warm the soup over low heat, then serve it immediately with toasted pumpkin seeds sprinkled on top.

Serves 8

Roast Loin of Pork
with Prunes, Apricots, and Madeira

I served this roast at dinner parties well before we became innkeepers. It is simple to prepare, and looks beautiful when carved.

1 pound large pitted prunes
Dry Madeira wine
15 large dried apricot halves
1 4- to 5-pound center loin
 pork roast, boned, rolled,
 and tied
½ teaspoon ground ginger

½ teaspoon salt
¼ teaspoon fresh-ground
 pepper
½ cup dry white wine
1 cup heavy cream
Salt and fresh-ground pepper
 to taste

In a medium bowl, combine the prunes with enough Madeira to cover. Let stand at room temperature for 3 hours.

Preheat the oven to 325°.

With a long, sharp knife, cut a lengthwise slit in the center of the roast. Using a wooden spoon handle, push a prune and then a pair of apricot halves into the cavity of the roast. Repeat until the cavity is completely filled, using all of the apricot halves; some prunes should be left over.

In a small bowl, combine the ginger, salt, and pepper. Rub the mixture all over the pork roast. Place the meat, fat side up, in a narrow, deep baking dish that holds the pork snugly (a bread pan works well). Place the pan in the oven, and roast for 30 minutes.

Drain the remaining prunes, reserving the Madeira. Mix the Madeira and white wine, and pour the wine mixture over the roast. Continue roasting the pork for 1 hour, basting it frequently with the pan juices. Add the cream, and continue roasting, basting frequently, for 45 minutes.

Remove the roast from the pan, and keep it warm. Skim off the fat from the pan. Over high heat, reduce the juices in the pan until they are thickened. Add the remaining prunes, and heat, stirring. Add salt and pepper. Keep the sauce warm.

Carve the pork roast into 1-inch slices, so that each slice shows a prune or an apricot in the center, and spoon some of the sauce over the slices. Serve immediately, with the remaining sauce on the side.

Serves 6 to 8

Individual Apple Tarts
with Maple Syrup and Vanilla Ice Cream

The first time we made these apple tarts we served them with just vanilla ice cream, and we all swooned. But as Ted was sitting in the kitchen tasting his, he came up with the idea of putting maple syrup on top. He was so excited by the result that he immediately filled a pitcher with maple syrup and walked around the dining room pouring some on everyone's tart. The combination of flavors was pure ecstasy.

1 pound frozen puff pastry, thawed

4 Granny Smith apples, peeled, cored, and sliced thin

4 tablespoons unsalted butter, cut into small pieces

4 tablespoons sugar
Vanilla ice cream
Pure maple syrup

Preheat the oven to 400°.

On a lightly floured work surface, roll out the dough ⅛-inch thick. Cut out four 7-inch rounds. Place the rounds on a large, heavy cookie sheet, spaced well apart.

Using one apple per tart, arrange the slices in concentric circles on the dough rounds. Dot each tart with 1 tablespoon butter, and sprinkle each tart with 1 tablespoon sugar.

Bake the tarts in the middle of the oven for 25 minutes, or until the pastry is golden brown.

Transfer the tarts to plates, and serve them warm with a scoop of vanilla ice cream and a little maple syrup poured over the ice cream.

Serves 4

WINTER DINNER

Goat Cheese Soufflé

Carrot and Chestnut Soup

Rock Cornish Hens with Champagne

Celery-Root Purée

Lemon Meringue Tart

WINTER IS THE TIME for settling in—for sitting by the fireside, cozy and warm, while a snowstorm blows outside. Actually, you don't even need a snowstorm—a good book will make you feel snug. But I truly love snow, the more the better. I love going for walks just after the snow has fallen, when everything is white, like a fairyland glistening in the sunlight. The world is so quiet, so peaceful.

Ted and I like to cross-country ski. Every winter, when it is the quietest at the inn, we say we will go cross-country skiing whenever it snows. But since we've become innkeepers we've been so involved in our winter projects that we have yet to ski at all!

For Christmas in 1991, Ted bought me two pairs of snow-shoes (it just so happened that one of the pairs fit him very well). Unfortunately, we did not have much snow that winter, so they have not been broken in yet.

Whether or not you enjoy winter sports, winter is time for the heartiest of foods. Winter is also the time for making dishes that may be a little more complicated than usual, because you don't mind spending more hours indoors. My favorite food to make in winter is bread. The smell of it baking! Even more wonderful is a buttered slice of bread still hot from the oven (Ted and I have been known to eat an entire loaf of fresh bread at a time). Homemade pizza is wonderful, too.

This winter menu has some of my other favorites. Soufflés are a joy to serve, Carrot and Chestnut Soup is a winter luxury, and Celery-Root Purée is heavenly. The hens in champagne will warm you to your toes, and the tart will surely make you pucker.

Goat Cheese Soufflé

I love serving soufflés, if not for dessert then as appetizers. This one is especially light and airy, and very impressive. Be sure to serve it as soon as it comes out of the oven.

1 cup walnut meats
1½ cups milk
4 tablespoons unsalted butter
4 tablespoons all-purpose flour
1 teaspoon cornstarch
6 eggs, separated

1½ cups crumbled mild goat cheese
2 tablespoons cognac
1½ teaspoons *herbes de Provence*
Fresh-ground black pepper to taste
Pinch cream of tartar

Preheat the oven to 350°. To toast the walnuts, spread them in one layer on a baking sheet. Place the baking sheet in the oven, and toast the walnuts for ten minutes. Remove the pan from the oven, and let the nuts cool. Chop them fine.

Butter well the bottoms and sides of eight soufflé cups, then coat the bottoms and sides with chopped walnuts. Reserve the remaining walnuts.

Heat the milk in a heavy saucepan, but do not let it boil.

Melt the butter over low heat in another heavy saucepan. Whisk in the flour and cornstarch and cook them, whisking constantly, for 3 minutes. Still whisking, slowly add the milk to the flour mixture. Bring to a boil, stirring constantly, then remove the pan from the heat. Transfer the mixture to a bowl, and let it cool slightly.

Set the oven to 400°.

Whisk the egg yolks into the cooled mixture, one at a time. Then add the goat cheese, cognac, *herbes de Provence*, and pepper, and whisk until all are combined.

Beat the egg whites with the cream of tartar just until they hold stiff peaks. Stir a fourth of the whites into the cheese mixture to lighten it. Gently fold in the remaining whites.

Divide the soufflé mixture among the soufflé cups, and

sprinkle each with about 1 tablespoon of the remaining walnuts. Bake the soufflés for 20 minutes, or until they are puffed
and golden brown. Serve them immediately.

Serves 8

Carrot and Chestnut Soup

We all love this soup because of its creamy texture and rich taste.

6 tablespoons unsalted butter
1 large onion, chopped
3 cups minced carrots
1 pound shelled chestnuts, chopped

5 cups chicken stock
¼ cup brandy
½ cup heavy cream
Fresh-ground pepper to taste
Crème fraîche (see page 31)

Melt the butter in a large saucepan. Add the chopped onion, and sauté until it is soft, about 5 minutes. Add the carrots, and sauté 5 minutes more. Add the chestnuts, and sauté for an additional 5 minutes.

Add the chicken stock and brandy, and bring to a boil. Reduce the heat, cover, and simmer for 30 minutes, stirring occasionally.

Purée the soup, in batches, in a food processor or blender, and return it to the saucepan. Add the heavy cream and pepper, and heat the soup over low heat (do not let it boil).

Serve the soup garnished with *crème fraîche*.

Serves 6

Rock Cornish Hens with Champagne

I serve half a hen per person as part of a five-course dinner. If you were serving only one course, you would want to serve a whole hen per person. The combination of flavors in the champagne sauce is wonderful.

¼ cup unsalted butter
¼ cup olive oil
4 Rock Cornish hens, split in half
1 large onion, minced
1 garlic clove, minced
½ cup cognac
3 tablespoons all-purpose flour

2 teaspoons crushed dried herbs (bay leaf, rosemary, tarragon, and thyme)
3½ cups champagne
1 pound mushrooms, sliced
1 cup *crème fraîche* (see page 31), at room temperature

In a large skillet, melt the butter with the olive oil over medium-high heat. Add the Rock Cornish hens, and sauté them until they are completely browned on both sides. With tongs, gently remove them from the skillet, and keep them warm.

Add the onion and garlic to the butter and olive oil in the pan, and sauté them until they are soft, about 5 minutes. Remove the pan from the heat, and drain off all but 1 tablespoon of the melted butter and olive oil remaining. Return the hens to the skillet, pour the cognac over them, and ignite the cognac by touching a lit match to the edge of the pan. Remove the hens, and keep them warm.

Add the flour and herbs to the skillet, and cook over low heat for 2 minutes, stirring constantly. Gradually whisk in 3 cups of champagne. Return the hens to the skillet, and coat them with the sauce. Cover the skillet, and simmer until the meat is tender, about 45 minutes. Remove the hens, and keep them warm.

Add the remaining ½ cup champagne to the skillet. Increase the heat to high, and cook until the liquid is reduced by half. Reduce the heat, add the mushrooms, and simmer for 10 minutes. Remove the skillet from the heat.

In a small bowl, whisk the *crème fraîche* until it is slightly runny. Add the *crème fraîche* to the skillet, stirring well to blend the sauce. Return the hens to the pan, and coat them well with the sauce. Transfer them to plates, ladle the sauce over, and serve the hens with Celery-Root Purée.

Serves 8

Celery-Root Purée

I used to think that plain mashed potatoes were the best "comfort food," until I combined them with celery root, or celeriac. When I serve this dish for dinner, I have to make extra so that all of us in the kitchen can indulge.

3 medium-large celery roots, peeled and cut into chunks
2 large potatoes, peeled and quartered
1 garlic clove, crushed

½ cup heavy cream
4 tablespoons butter, at room temperature
Salt to taste
Fresh-ground white pepper to taste

Combine the celery root, potatoes, and garlic in a large saucepan. Cover them with cold water. Bring the water to a boil, and simmer, covered, for 30 minutes, until the celery root and potatoes are tender.

Drain the vegetables well, and return them to the saucepan. Add the heavy cream, and cook, stirring constantly, until the liquid is evaporated.

Transfer the mixture to a food processor, add the butter, and purée. Add salt and pepper, and serve the purée immediately.

Serves 4 to 6

Lemon Meringue Tart

This is for the true lemon lover. It is *really* lemony—a tart tart!

FOR THE PASTRY:
1 cup all-purpose flour
2 tablespoons sugar
Pinch salt
½ cup (¼ pound) unsalted
   butter, chilled and cut
   into ½-inch pieces

1 egg yolk
1 tablespoon heavy cream
Rind of 1 lemon, grated fine

FOR THE FILLING:
2 eggs
2 egg yolks
¾ cup sugar
⅔ cup fresh lemon juice
Rind of 2 lemons, grated fine

½ cup (¼ pound) unsalted
   butter, at room temperature, cut into pieces

FOR THE MERINGUE:
Zest of 1 lemon, removed in
   thin strips with a
   vegetable peeler
¼ cup fresh lemon juice

⅓ cup plus 3 tablespoons
   sugar
3 egg whites, at room
   temperature

Make the tart shell: Combine the flour, sugar, and salt. Cut in the butter until the mixture resembles coarse meal. In a small bowl, whisk together the egg yolk, the cream, and the lemon rind. Lightly stir the liquid into the flour-butter mixture until the dough is just blended.

Turn the dough out on a work surface, and briefly knead it until it holds together. Form the dough into a ball. Wrap it, and refrigerate it for 30 minutes.

Roll the dough out on a floured surface. Line a 9-inch tart pan with the dough, leaving a ½-inch border above the rim of the pan. Prick the dough all over with a fork. Chill the shell for 30 minutes.

Preheat the oven to 375°. Line the shell with foil, fill the foil with dried beans, and bake the shell for 15 minutes. Remove the beans and foil, and bake the shell 10 minutes more, or until it is pale golden. Place the pan on a rack, and let the shell cool.

Make the filling: In a small, heavy saucepan, whisk together the eggs, egg yolks and sugar until the mixture is well combined. Whisk in the lemon juice and rind. Over low heat, continue to whisk until the mixture is very thick, approximately 10 minutes.

Remove the pan from the heat, and whisk in the butter, a few pieces at a time. Scrape the mixture into the cooled tart shell, and smooth the top with a spatula. Let the tart cool, then refrigerate it until the filling is firm, about 4 hours.

Make the meringue: In a heavy saucepan, combine the strips of lemon, the lemon juice, and ⅓ cup sugar. Bring the mixture to a boil, stirring until the sugar is dissolved, then simmer gently for 15 minutes.

In a bowl, beat the whites until they just hold soft peaks. Beat in the remaining 3 tablespoons sugar, and continue beating until the meringue just holds stiff peaks. Remove the zest from the syrup, and add the hot syrup to the meringue in a stream while beating constantly. Continue to beat the meringue until it is cool.

Spread the meringue over the lemon filling, covering the filling completely. Using a propane torch or broiler, brown the meringue, being careful not to burn it. Chill the tart for 2 hours before serving.

Serves 8

GREEK DINNER

Tiropitakia (Cheese-filled Triangles)

Spanakopita (Spinach and Cheese Pie)

Chicken Soup with *Avgolemono* (Egg and Lemon) Sauce

Greek Twist Bread

George's Greek Lamb

Sautéed Zucchini in Tomato Sauce

Kadayif with Cream Filling

I AM OF 100 PERCENT Greek heritage. As I was growing up, my life was filled with Mediterranean traditions, most of which involved food.

My fondest memories are of our Eastern Orthodox Easter. Throughout Lent, the special *halvahs* (pistachio was my favorite) would arrive at my dad's store. During this time, too, we would eat wonderful bean soups. The week before Easter was really hectic, both at home and at the store. On Palm Sunday, the entire family—grandparents, aunts, uncles, and cousins—would all become involved in dyeing eggs red to sell at the store. Dozens and dozens of eggs would be dyed, all of them ordered by our customers in advance.

Because my father sold lamb, we would have all the ingredients necessary for a real Greek Easter dinner, from lambs' heads to be roasted (although I would never even try one) to the heart, liver, lung, and intestines for the special Easter soup served Saturday at midnight (I wouldn't try the soup, either). It was hard for me to handle some of those foods, let alone to eat them!

On Good Friday we would fast the entire day, and on Saturday morning we would all go to communion. After communion, we would have a special breakfast at church, featuring chocolate milk and the most wonderful hot cross buns I can remember. Then it would be back to work at the store.

Good Friday and the Saturday before Easter were always the two busiest days at my father's store. We would work very long days the entire Holy Week, but Friday and Saturday were completely exhausting—especially after my dad came down with his "Easteritis," another tradition at Easter. Every year, on either Good Friday or the day after, his right arm would swell up from cutting so much lamb. Then he would get a fever, and we would have to send him home.

The finest celebration of all, our Easter dinner always started with the cracking of the Easter eggs. There was one red-dyed egg for each person. We would take turns hitting eggs against each other, and the last person with an uncracked egg would have good luck until the next Easter. We would then eat the most glorious of dinners, including leg of lamb, little red potatoes, fresh asparagus, Greek bread, Greek salad, the most wonderful homemade yogurt, which my mother had made the day before, and spinach pie. For dessert we usually had something light with lemon, such as a soufflé. Then more relatives would come for coffee, and we would bring out more pastries, desserts, and the traditional Easter cookie, the *koulourakia*. When my grandmother was alive, she would make my all-time favorite pastry, *thiples*, a crisp fried dough dipped in honey syrup.

I hope you find this menu exotic and fun. Enjoy it with a nice bottle of Greek retsina wine.

Tiropitakia
(Cheese-filled Triangles)

These buttery, cheese-filled hors d'oeuvres are wonderful served directly from the oven while still warm and puffed. They can also be made ahead and frozen for later use.

1 pound feta cheese
8 ounces cottage cheese
4 ounces cream cheese
3 eggs, lightly beaten
Fresh-ground pepper to taste
½ cup (¼ pound) unsalted
   butter

1 pound phyllo dough
   (available in the freezer
   section of most
   supermarkets), thawed in
   the refrigerator

In a bowl, crumble the feta cheese with a fork. Blend in the cottage and cream cheeses. Add the eggs and pepper, and mix well.

In a small saucepan, melt the butter.

Cut the stack of phyllo dough into thirds lengthwise. Use one third at a time, keeping the rest under a damp towel.

Brush one strip of phyllo dough with the melted butter. Lay a second strip over the first, and brush again with the butter. Place a heaping tablespoon of the cheese mixture in a corner at one end of the strip, and fold the dough over and over in a triangle shape, as one folds a flag. Continue folding to the end of the phyllo strip. Place the triangle on an ungreased baking sheet. Repeat with the remaining phyllo and filling. At this point the *tiropitakias* can be frozen for later use. Freeze them on the baking sheet before transferring them to freezer containers.

To bake fresh *tiropitakias*, preheat the oven to 375°. Brush the tops of the pastries with melted butter. Bake them 15 minutes, or until they are golden brown. (Bake frozen *tiropitakias* at 400° for 20 minutes.)

Serve the baked *tiropitakias* immediately.

Makes approximately 48 triangles

Spanakopita
(Spinach and Cheese Pie)

Spanakopita is traditionally eaten either before or during dinner. I prefer to serve it as a first course in a five-course dinner.

1 bunch scallions, chopped
1 cup (½ pound) plus 2 tablespoons unsalted butter
2 pounds spinach, leaves only, washed and drained
6 eggs, lightly beaten
1 pound feta cheese, crumbled
12 ounces cottage cheese
2 tablespoons dry bread crumbs

½ cup chopped Italian parsley
½ cup minced fresh dill
Salt and fresh-ground pepper to taste
1 pound phyllo dough (available in the freezer section of most supermarkets), thawed in the refrigerator

In a small pan, sauté the scallions in 2 tablespoons butter until they are soft.

Chop the spinach and place it in a large skillet. Cover, and cook until the spinach is wilted. Drain the spinach in a sieve, pressing out as much moisture as possible with the back of a spoon.

Grease well a 9-by-13-inch baking pan. Preheat the oven to 350°.

Mix together the scallions, spinach, eggs, feta and cottage cheeses, bread crumbs, parsley, and dill. Season the mixture lightly with salt and pepper.

In a small pan, melt the remaining butter. Unfold the phyllo pastry, and lay one sheet on the bottom of the 9-by-13-inch pan, keeping the remainder covered with a damp towel. Brush the phyllo sheet with melted butter. Lay another sheet of phyllo over the first, brush it, and repeat until half the phyllo dough has been used. Then spread the spinach mixture evenly over the dough, lay a phyllo sheet over, and butter the sheet. Continue layering the phyllo and melted butter until all the phyllo is used up.

Using a sharp razor blade (or a sharp, pointed knife), score the top two or three layers of phyllo dough into 3-inch squares.

Place the pan in the oven, and bake the *spanakopita* for 1 hour, or until it is golden brown. Let it stand for 20 minutes before serving.

Serves 12

Chicken Soup
with *Avgolemono* (Egg and Lemon) Sauce

This soup is my favorite of all Greek dishes. To me, it ranks with mashed potatoes and celery-root purée as sublime comfort food.

6 cups chicken stock
½ cup uncooked rice
4 eggs, separated

Juice of 2 lemons
Fresh-ground pepper to taste

In a kettle, bring the chicken stock to a boil. Add the rice, cover the kettle, and gently boil for 18 minutes.

Remove the kettle from the heat. Measure 2 cups of the stock. Cover the remaining stock and rice, and keep hot.

In a large mixing bowl, beat the egg whites until they are stiff. Add the egg yolks one at a time, beating well after each addition. Very, very slowly add the 2 cups hot chicken stock to the egg mixture, beating continuously. Beat until the mixture is frothy, approximately 5 minutes. Then add the lemon juice very slowly, while continuing to beat.

Stirring constantly, pour the egg-lemon sauce slowly into the soup. Blend thoroughly.

Serve the soup immediately, with a little pepper over each serving.

Serves 8

Greek Twist Bread

The special ingredient in this bread is *masticha*, a sweet flavoring derived from the sap of the mastic tree, which grows only on the Greek island of Chios. *Masticha* is also used in cakes, cookies, candies, drinks, and liqueurs. It is hard to find, but worth the search. You will never forget the aroma as it is cooking, nor will you ever forget its taste.

3 tablespoons dry yeast	¼ cup orange juice
1 cup milk	1 tablespoon *masticha*,
1 cup sugar	ground
7 cups all-purpose flour	4 tablespoons light cream
¾ cup unsalted butter	1 egg yolk
3 eggs, well beaten	Sesame seeds

Dissolve the yeast in 1 cup lukewarm water. Scald the milk, and let it cool to lukewarm.

Combine the yeast and 1 teaspoon of the sugar in a large bowl. Stir in the milk. Add 2 cups of the flour, and mix completely. Cover the bowl with a cloth, and let the sponge rise in a warm place about one and a half hours, until it is doubled in bulk.

In another bowl, cream the butter and remaining sugar. Add the eggs, orange juice, and *masticha*, and mix completely. Add the risen sponge, and stir until blended. Stir in the remaining flour. Knead the dough until it is smooth, about 10 minutes.

Place the dough in a well-greased bowl, and turn the dough to grease its entire surface. Cover the bowl tightly with plastic wrap, and then wrap the bowl in a large towel. Place the bowl in a warm, draft-free place, and let the dough rise until it has doubled in bulk, approximately one and a half hours.

Grease well two 9-inch cake pans.

Turn the dough out on a floured board, and knead it lightly. Cut the dough in half. Cut each half into three pieces, and roll each piece to a cylinder approximately 10 inches long. Braid the three pieces together, then bend the dough into a circle and place it in a cake pan. Repeat this with the remaining dough.

Cover the dough with a towel, and place it in a warm place

to rise for about one and a half hours, until it is doubled in bulk.

Preheat the oven to 350°.

In a small bowl, combine the cream and egg yolk. Brush the tops of the loaves with this mixture, then sprinkle the loaves with sesame seeds.

Bake the bread for 45 minutes. After 25 minutes, check whether the tops of the loaves are brown. If they are, cover the loaves with aluminum foil for the remainder of the cooking time.

Remove the pans from the oven, and remove the loaves from the pans. Allow the bread to cool completely before serving.

Makes 2 loaves

George's Greek Lamb

George is my dad, who taught me how to make this dish. It is the first dish I ever entered in a cooking contest. I had never been so nervous. The food had to be prepared in a school kitchen, and we couldn't see the judges tasting it. I gave the presenters strict instructions not to open the paper until the dish was in front of the judges, so the judges could appreciate those aromas as the paper was being cut. This must have worked, because I won first prize. This lamb dish is always very popular at the inn.

1 6- to 7-pound leg of lamb, boned, butterflied, and cut in half lengthwise
2 garlic cloves, sliced
Juice of 1 lemon
1 tablespoon dried oregano leaves
Salt and fresh-ground pepper to taste
1 pound *kasseri* cheese (available in Greek groceries, cheese shops, and some supermarkets)

Preheat the oven to 350°.

Rub the meat with the lemon juice, oregano, salt, and pepper. On each piece, make incisions with a pointed knife, and insert the slices of garlic.

Cut the *kasseri* cheese into strips ½-inch thick and 1-inch wide. Place the cheese on one half of the lamb. Place the cheese-covered lamb on a piece of parchment paper long enough to wrap both pieces of meat (about 25 inches long). Then place the other piece of lamb on top of the cheese, and cover with the paper, folding the two ends together. Wrap the meat again in two sheets of parchment paper. Wrap it again, like a parcel, in a piece of brown kraft paper (a paper grocery bag cut open), and tie it well with cotton string.

Place the parcel on a rack in a baking pan, with enough water just to reach the bottom of the paper. Roast 2 hours. If the paper begins to burn, turn the parcel over in the pan. Add water to the pan as needed.

Remove the roast from the oven, and immediately bring it to the table in its wrappings. Let all present smell the incredible aromas as the paper is cut.

Serves 8

Sautéed Zucchini in Tomato Sauce

Most Greek vegetable preparations include onions and tomatoes, and this one is no exception. For some of us, adding a loaf of bread and some Greek feta cheese to this dish would make it a complete meal.

1 pound small zucchini,
  sliced in ¼-inch rounds
Salt and fresh-ground pepper
  to taste
¼ cup olive oil
2 medium onions, chopped

2 garlic cloves, minced
1 tablespoon cornstarch
1½ cups canned tomatoes,
  chopped
1 cup tomato purée
Juice of ½ lemon

Sprinkle the zucchini pieces with salt and pepper.

In a large skillet, heat the olive oil. Add the zucchini slices, and sauté them until they are lightly browned. Remove the zucchini from the skillet with a slotted spoon. Add the onions and garlic to the skillet, and cook them over medium heat until they are soft, approximately 10 minutes.

In a small bowl, mix the cornstarch with 1 tablespoon water. Add the cornstarch mixture to the skillet with the tomatoes, tomato purée, and lemon juice. Simmer, stirring occasionally, for 10 minutes, or until the sauce is slightly thickened.

Add the zucchini to the skillet, and stir thoroughly. Cook over low heat for an additional 10 minutes. Taste for seasoning, and add salt and pepper if needed. Serve immediately.

Serves 6

Kadayif with Cream Filling

Being a custard fan, I am partial to this simple dessert, a marvelous alternative to baklava. *Kadayif* dough is a special shredded phyllo; there is no substitute.

2 cups heavy cream
2 cups light cream
½ cup sugar
1 cup milk
½ cup cornstarch
2 pounds *kadayif* (available in Greek or Armenian groceries)

2 cups (1 pound) unsalted butter
3 cups sugar
1 teaspoon lemon juice

Prepare the cream filling several hours ahead: Mix the heavy and light creams with ½ cup sugar in a deep saucepan. As the mixture is heating, combine the milk with the cornstarch in a jar, and shake well until the cornstarch is completely dissolved. Pour the cornstarch mixture slowly into the hot cream mixture, stirring continuously until the cream thickens. Bring the mixture to a boil, and simmer 2 minutes. Pour the mixture into a large bowl, and let it cool.

Preheat the oven to 400°.

Separate and loosen shreds of the *kadayif* by rubbing gently; collect the shreds in a bowl. Melt the butter in a small pan over low heat, and pour it over the *kadayif*. Blend thoroughly by tossing the *kadayif* gently. Divide the mixture in half. Spread one-half in a 12-by-16-inch baking pan. Gently press down.

Spread the cream filling evenly over the *kadayif*, keeping it ¼ inch away from the edge of the pan. Cover the filling with the other half of the *kadayif*, and press down gently. Bake the *kadayif* 30 minutes, or until it is golden brown. Let it cool in the pan.

In a small saucepan, bring the sugar, ½ cup water, and the lemon juice to a rolling boil, then remove the pan from the heat. Let the syrup stand until it is lukewarm. Pour it over the *kadayif*, and let the *kadayif* rest at least 30 to 60 minutes before serving.

The *kadayif* may be refrigerated overnight.

Serves 12

ITALIAN DINNER

Baked Polenta with Cheese (and Variations)

Tuscan Bean and Vegetable Soup

Chicken Breasts with Prosciutto and Marsala

Sautéed Spinach with Garlic

Tiramisù

TED HAS ALWAYS SAID that he must be half Italian. I think many Americans feel this way. As I was growing up, if my mother was not cooking Greek, she was cooking Italian. On Sundays our big meal was at 1:00, so in the evenings we would usually call the local pizzeria—for handmade pizzas, not the fast-food variety.

When I was in my early twenties, I spent two weeks in Italy. I remember all the sights and the excitement of being there, but what I remember best is the delicious, uncomplicated, down-to-earth food. This is the kind of food I like to cook.

I feel more passionate about Italian food than about any other kind. Always at hand in my kitchen are pasta, Arborio rice, mascarpone cheese, porcini mushrooms, cornmeal for polenta, a lot of garlic, Parmesan cheese, olive oil, prosciutto, sun-dried tomatoes, *pignoli* (pine nuts), and Marsala wine, so that at any time I can cook Italian.

It seems we receive the most compliments when we serve Italian specialties, whether risotto, pasta, polenta, *tiramisù*, or *semifreddo*. And even when the names of the dishes aren't Italian, the Italian influence always shows up in my menus.

Baked Polenta with Cheese (and Variations)

Our guests love polenta, and I appreciate its versatility. It can be served either as mush or baked, with any number of added ingredients. Polenta is also easy to prepare, and it can be made ahead and baked at the last minute. We serve it as a first course.

BASIC RECIPE:

4 cups chicken stock

3 tablespoons unsalted butter

1 cup coarse-ground yellow cornmeal

½ cup freshly grated Parmesan cheese

In a heavy kettle, bring the stock to a boil with the butter. Add the cornmeal in a slow stream, while whisking. Whisk the mixture over low heat for 15 minutes, or until it is very thick. Gradually whisk in the Parmesan cheese, and continue whisking until the cheese is completely melted.

Pour the mixture into a well-buttered, 8-inch-wide deep-dish pie plate. Let the polenta cool completely at room temperature, and then refrigerate it for at least 4 hours, preferably overnight.

Preheat the oven to 375°. Line a baking sheet with parchment paper. Cut the polenta into eight wedges, and lay them on the parchment paper. Bake 15 minutes, then serve them immediately.

VARIATIONS:

1. Serve the baked polenta basic recipe with a simple tomato sauce made from fresh tomatoes.

2. Before baking the polenta, sprinkle the tops of the wedges with additional Parmesan cheese and fresh-ground black pepper.

3. Before baking the polenta, sprinkle the wedges with additional Parmesan cheese, and top with thin slices of fontina cheese. Bake until the cheeses are melted through, approximately 15 minutes.

Serve at once with Porcini Mushroom Sauce: Heat ¼ cup olive oil in a large skillet. Add three cloves garlic, minced, and sauté, stirring, for 2 minutes. Add 1½ pounds fresh porcini mushrooms, sliced ½-inch thick, and sauté, stirring, for 5 minutes. Season with salt and fresh-ground pepper to taste. Serve immediately.

4. Polenta with Leeks, Bacon, and Goat Cheese: In a skillet, cook four slices lean bacon, chopped, with 1 tablespoon olive oil until the bacon is crisp. Add one garlic clove, minced, and ¼ cup chopped leeks, white part only. Sauté until the leeks are soft. Add the bacon mixture and ½ cup crumbled goat cheese to the basic polenta mixture before pouring it into the 8-inch pie plate. Proceed with the basic recipe. Serve the baked polenta with a simple tomato sauce.

Serves 8

Tuscan Bean and Vegetable Soup

Although we serve it in small bowls for our soup course, this soup is hearty and satisfying on its own, for lunch or dinner. I can't think of anything better on a cold winter evening than a large bowl of this soup with a loaf of freshly baked Italian bread.

The recipe can be halved.

1 pound small navy beans
14 cups beef stock
3 tablespoons olive oil
3 ounces prosciutto, chopped
½ cup chopped Italian parsley
2 garlic cloves, minced
2 large carrots, coarsely chopped
2 large onions, coarsely chopped
1 fennel bulb, coarsely chopped
2 pounds savoy cabbage, shredded
¼ cup tomato paste
½ teaspoon crushed red pepper flakes
1 bay leaf
½ cup long-grain rice
Fresh-grated Parmesan cheese

Put the beans and beef stock in a kettle, and bring the stock to a boil. Reduce the heat, and simmer for 1 hour and 15 minutes, or until the beans are tender.

Meanwhile, heat the olive oil in a large skillet. Add the prosciutto, parsley, and garlic, and sauté, stirring frequently, for 10 minutes. Add the carrots, onions, and fennel, and continue to sauté, stirring frequently, for an additional 10 minutes. Add the cabbage, tomato paste, and crushed red peppers, and sauté, stirring frequently, for 5 minutes more.

Add the sautéed vegetables and the bay leaf to the kettle. There should be enough stock in the pot to cover the vegetables; if not, add more stock. Bring the soup to a boil. Add the rice, stirring with a wooden spoon. Cover the pot, turn the heat down to medium-low, and cook for 17 minutes, stirring often.

Serve the soup hot, sprinkled with the grated Parmesan cheese.

Serves 12

Chicken Breasts with Prosciutto and Marsala

When we cook this dish, with its combination of porcini mushrooms, prosciutto, and Marsala, the aromas wafting through the kitchen are just incredible. The first time we served this dish, a guest said he would walk a mile for it.

2 ounces dried porcini mushrooms

4 whole chicken breasts, boned and skinned

Flour seasoned with salt and pepper, for dredging

3 tablespoons olive oil

4 tablespoons butter

½ pound fresh mushrooms, quartered

½ cup Marsala wine

4 ounces prosciutto, cut into julienne strips

Combine the porcini mushrooms in a small bowl with enough hot water just to cover them. Let them soften about 30 minutes.

Drain the porcini mushrooms in a sieve lined with dampened paper towels and set over a small bowl. Rinse the porcini mushrooms with cold water, to remove any remaining dirt or sand, and pat them dry. Chop them coarsely. Set the soaking liquid aside.

Dredge the chicken lightly in the seasoned flour. Preheat the oven to 250°. In a large skillet, heat the olive oil and butter over medium-high heat, and in it sauté the chicken breasts for 3 minutes on each side, or until they are lightly browned. Transfer the chicken to a plate, and keep it warm in the oven.

Add the porcini and fresh mushrooms to the skillet, and sauté them, stirring frequently, over medium-high heat for 5 minutes. Pour in the Marsala wine and ½ cup of the reserved mushroom liquid. Bring the liquid to a boil, and simmer for 5 minutes, or until the sauce is slightly thickened.

Add to the skillet the prosciutto and the chicken, with any juices that have accumulated on the plate. Simmer the mixture, covered, for 15 minutes, or until the chicken is cooked through.

Divide the chicken among four plates, season with salt and pepper, and spoon the prosciutto and mushroom sauce on top. Serve immediately.

Serves 4

Sautéed Spinach with Garlic

It amazes me how often guests comment when we serve this spinach—they just love it, especially because of all the garlic. Many of us tend to use spinach mostly in salads, but try this dish and you'll be a fan of cooked spinach.

Pinch salt
1½ pounds fresh spinach, leaves only, washed and drained

2 tablespoons olive oil
4 garlic cloves, sliced
Salt and fresh-ground pepper to taste

In a saucepan, heat 2 cups water with a pinch of salt. When the water comes to a boil, add the spinach leaves. Stir to immerse all the leaves. Bring the water to a second boil, and simmer the spinach for 5 minutes. Immediately place the pan in the sink and run cold water into it.

Transfer the spinach to a strainer. Press the spinach with the back of a spoon to extract as much of the liquid as possible. Chop the spinach coarsely.

Heat the olive oil in a skillet. Add the garlic slices, and sauté them just until they begin to brown. Add the spinach, and sauté for 4 minutes, stirring frequently.

Season the spinach with salt and pepper, and serve it immediately.

Serves 4

Tiramisù

Tiramisù (which means "pick me up") is a very old, simple dessert first created in Venice. In recent years, it has become very stylish in this country. This is one of those desserts to die for.

3 egg yolks
3 tablespoons sugar
⅔ cup Marsala wine
⅔ cup very strong espresso
   coffee, cold

8 ounces mascarpone cheese
1¼ cups heavy cream
12 ladyfingers
3 tablespoons unsweetened
   cocoa powder

In a large mixing bowl, whisk the egg yolks and sugar until the mixture is very thick, approximately 10 minutes. Add ⅓ cup of the Marsala, and continue whisking until the mixture is again very thick.

Stir ⅓ cup of the espresso coffee into the mascarpone cheese until they are well blended.

Beat the heavy cream until soft peaks form.

Combine the remaining Marsala and espresso coffee in a pie plate. Dip the ladyfingers into the coffee mixture, then place two ladyfingers in each of six large wine glasses. Cover them first with the egg-yolk mixture, then the mascarpone mixture. Then divide the whipped cream among the wine glasses. Sprinkle the cocoa powder through a fine sieve over the glasses.

Chill the *tiramisù* for six hours before serving.

Serves 6

DO-AHEAD DINNER

Onion Tart

Celery Consommé

Grey Sole in Parchment Paper

Sautéed Vegetables

Bittersweet Chocolate Soufflés
with White Chocolate and Rum Sauce

WITH THE EXCEPTION of the Onion Tart, this menu was created for my first "Cooking with Chris" weekend at the inn. I planned the menu to show those attending that most of the work of making dinner could be done early in the day, enabling the cook to spend the evening with the guests, instead of in the kitchen.

I also wanted to alleviate the fear many people feel about preparing and serving certain foods. Whenever we serve a soufflé at the inn—for breakfast, as a first course, or as a dessert—I am asked at every table I visit how I dare make soufflés for all those people, and why they don't fall. I say I just do it and don't worry about it. There are times when the twenty-fourth soufflé we serve has started to settle a bit, but that is the nature of a soufflé. I am also asked about the adage that walking about the kitchen while a soufflé is baking will make it fall. Of course, we can't all leave the kitchen while the soufflés bake. If walking in the kitchen is so risky, I must have great luck.

As for consommés, I used to think they were something I

could not make. But a few years ago I tried this celery consommé, and I have loved making consommés ever since. I can remember that first time, putting the egg whites and shells into the soup and thinking it would never work. But we watched every step that day, and we were truly amazed at the end result—the most beautiful, clear soup we had ever seen, with slivers of carrots and celery floating in the bowls. Now when I make consommé, I call in whoever is around to watch me adding egg whites and shells to the soup. I say I am amazed that they have never had soup with egg shells in it before. I love the look on their faces at the end result.

The Grey Sole in Parchment uses two techniques I wanted to teach in the class. The first was peeling, seeding, and chopping tomatoes, and the second was using parchment paper. Neither process is difficult, but both can be a bit scary if you have never performed them before.

The Onion Tart is really not difficult if you use purchased puff pastry. The onion mixture can be made before your guests arrive, and all that has to be done while you and your guests enjoy the evening is the final hour of baking. *Gourmet* magazine asked me for this recipe.

I hope you enjoy my do-ahead menu. As I told my class the first time, just relax—you can do it.

Onion Tart

We have been serving this appetizer since we first started serving dinners, and it is still one of our most popular first courses.

4 large Spanish onions (or Vidalia onions, when in season), peeled and sliced thin
10 tablespoons unsalted butter
Salt and fresh-ground pepper to taste

⅓ pound puff pastry (thawed, if purchased frozen)
1 tablespoon whole-grain mustard
3 egg yolks
¼ cup heavy cream

Melt the butter in a large skillet over low heat. Add the onions, and stir well to coat them. Cover the skillet, and cook the onions over low heat for 10 minutes. Remove the cover, raise the heat to medium-high, and sauté the onions, stirring occasionally, until they are tender and just beginning to turn golden brown, approximately 25 minutes. Season with salt and pepper.

While the onions are cooking, preheat the oven to 375°. Roll out the puff pastry to a ⅛-inch thickness. Place it in an 11-inch tart pan, and crimp the edges. Line the pastry with aluminum foil, and fill it with dried beans or pie weights. Bake the tart shell for 25 minutes. Remove the weights and foil.

Spread the mustard over the bottom of the baked shell. Stir the egg yolks and cream into the onions. Pour the mixture into the prepared pastry shell. Bake the tart for another 30 minutes.

Remove the tart from the oven. Slice it into eight pieces, and garnish them with chives (preferably with blossoms). Serve immediately.

Serves 8

Celery Consommé

When we received our four stars from the *Maine Sunday Telegram*, the reviewer said this soup was "one of the clearest consommés I've ever seen. Like liquid gold, this perfectly clarified broth ... was captivating." That says it all!

11 cups chicken stock,
  homemade or canned
1 cup dry white wine
2 bunches celery, chopped,
  including leafy tops
2 onions, sliced thin
2 leeks, sliced thin

2 carrots, chopped
1 tablespoon dried tarragon
4 egg whites, lightly beaten
Shells of 4 washed eggs,
  crushed
½ cup julienned celery
½ cup julienned carrots

In a large kettle, combine the stock, the wine, half the chopped celery, and all the onions, leeks, and carrots. Bring the mixture to a boil, and simmer, covered, for 30 minutes.

Strain the mixture through a fine sieve set over a large bowl, pressing hard on the vegetables to extract their liquids, and return the broth to the pot. Add the second bunch of celery, the tarragon, and the egg whites and shells. Heat the broth, stirring, until it starts to boil, then immediately reduce the heat. Cook the soup at a bare simmer, undisturbed, for 20 minutes. Strain the soup through a fine sieve lined with dampened paper towels and set over a large bowl, and discard the solids.

For garnish, blanch the julienned celery and carrots in boiling salted water for 1 minute, and drain. Place the julienned celery and carrots in bowls, and ladle in the soup. Serve immediately.

Serves 10

Grey Sole in Parchment

This is one of our most popular fish entrées, and it's wonderful to make ahead for a dinner party. Parchment paper is available in kitchen specialty shops and some supermarkets. Food steamed in parchment is both flavorful and healthful.

½ pound fresh shiitake
   mushrooms, sliced ½-inch
   thick
¼ cup olive oil
1 pound tomatoes, peeled,
   seeded, and chopped
¾ cup *crème fraîche* (see
   page 31)

1 tablespoon coarse-grain
   mustard
Salt and fresh-ground pepper
   to taste
1½ pounds grey sole fillets

Sauté the mushrooms briefly in the oil. Add the tomatoes, and cook until the mixture is nearly dry. Let it cool.

In a small bowl, stir together the *crème fraîche*, mustard, salt, and pepper, and then stir this mixture into the tomato mixture.

Preheat the oven to 500°. Take six 11-by-15-inch sheets of parchment, and fold each sheet in half. Divide the fillets among the six sheets of parchment, placing the fillets inside against the fold. Divide the sauce among the fish packages, spreading it over the fillets. Seal the fillets in the parchment by rolling the cut edges toward the fish. Place the packages on a cookie sheet, and bake them 10 minutes, or until they puff.

Serve the packages unopened so your guests can fully enjoy the fragrance that will rise as they cut through the parchment.

Serves 6

Sautéed Vegetables

As part of your do-ahead menu, the vegetables can all be cut up a few hours ahead and kept in plastic bags in the refrigerator.

4 carrots, cut in ⅛-inch diagonal slices
Pinch salt
6 tablespoons unsalted butter
1 medium onion, chopped
1 garlic clove, minced
1 large shallot, minced
4 small zucchini, cut in ⅛-inch diagonal slices
½ pound fresh shiitake mushrooms, sliced ¼-inch thick
1 red bell pepper, cut into julienne strips
½ pound snow peas, strings removed
1 teaspoon raspberry vinegar
Salt and fresh-ground pepper to taste

Bring a small pan of water to a boil. Add a pinch of salt and the carrots. Blanch the carrots for 4 minutes. Remove the pan from the heat, and drain the carrots. Immerse them in ice water for 2 minutes to stop the cooking. Drain them well.

Melt the butter in a large skillet. Add the onion, garlic, and shallot, and sauté 3 minutes. Add the blanched carrots, and sauté 5 minutes. Add the zucchini and mushrooms, and continue to sauté for another 5 minutes. Add the red bell pepper, snow peas, and raspberry vinegar, and sauté 3 minutes more.

Season the vegetables with salt and pepper to taste, and serve them immediately.

Serves 6

Bittersweet Chocolate Soufflés
with White Chocolate and Rum Sauce

If you prepare the soufflés in the afternoon, you can bake them
while the dishes are being cleared and coffee is being served.
Your dinner guests will think you are truly magical.

8 ounces semisweet
   chocolate, chopped
1 tablespoon unsalted butter
1 tablespoon all-purpose
   flour
½ cup milk
3 egg yolks

1 teaspoon vanilla extract
4 egg whites
1 teaspoon lemon juice
¼ cup sugar
Confectioner's sugar
White Chocolate and Rum
   Sauce (recipe follows)

Lightly butter eight 6-ounce ramekins, and dust them well
with granulated sugar. Set them aside.

Melt the chocolate in a double boiler, covered, over barely
simmering water. Remove the cover, and stir until the chocolate is smooth. Remove the top pan of the double boiler from
the heat.

In a small saucepan, melt the butter over moderate heat.
Stir in the flour, and cook until the mixture is thickened but
not browned, 1 to 2 minutes. Add the milk, and whisk briskly
until the mixture is smooth and thick, about 3 minutes. Remove the pan from the heat, add the melted chocolate, and
whisk until smooth. Whisk in the egg yolks and vanilla, and
set the pan aside.

Beat the egg whites and lemon juice at medium speed until
soft peaks form, about 1 minute. Gradually sprinkle the granulated sugar on top; continue to beat at high speed until the
whites are stiff but not dry. Using a rubber spatula, stir one-
quarter of the whites into the chocolate mixture to lighten it,
then fold in the remaining whites. Spoon the mixture into the
ramekins, filling each to the top.

At this point the soufflés can be refrigerated, uncovered, for
up to 5 hours.

Preheat the oven to 375°. Bake the soufflés for 17 minutes,
or until they are puffed and slightly cracked. Dust them with

confectioner's sugar, and serve them immediately. Pass a pitcher of the White Chocolate and Rum Sauce.

Serves 8

FOR THE WHITE CHOCOLATE AND RUM SAUCE:

6 ounces white chocolate, chopped

⅓ cup dark rum

In the top of a double boiler, slowly melt the white chocolate over simmering water. Whisk in the rum until it is completely incorporated. Remove the top of the double boiler from the heat, and let the sauce stand at room temperature.

The sauce may be served at room temperature or slightly warm.

VALENTINE'S DAY DINNER

Red Potatoes with *Crème Fraîche* and Caviar

Purée of Wild Mushroom Soup

Tenderloin of Beef with Horseradish Sauce

Chocolate Mousse Rum Cake

FOR THE PAST THREE YEARS we have offered a Valentine's Day weekend. Each year it has been one of our most popular weekends. We make it special by putting roses, champagne, candles, and heart-shaped boxes of chocolates in the rooms for our guests. For breakfast on Valentine's Day, we serve our guests heart-shaped scones and scrambled eggs with caviar in puff pastry.

Valentine's Day dinner is one of the most popular at the inn, second only to New Year's Eve. I think our dining room is the perfect setting, with red roses on the tables, red tablecloths on top of the white ones, and even red curtains. Large red heart doilies under the glass soup bowls, if I am serving a consommé, or beneath the dessert, are an added bit of whimsy for this special night. The dimmed electric lights, the candlelight, and the soft music make for a romantic evening out for our dinner guests.

The two foods that I must always have on my Valentine's Day menu are caviar, for the first course, and chocolate, for dessert.

The menu I have included for this dinner has both simple and complicated components. The first course and entrée are easier to prepare than the dessert. But for Valentine's Day, the dessert should be very special—and this one is.

Red Potatoes with
Crème Fraîche and Caviar

This is wonderfully simple, both in taste and in preparation. But its simplicity is matched by its elegance.

Small red potatoes (4 or 5   Caviar, black or red
  per serving)
Crème fraîche (see page 31)

    Gently scrub the potatoes to remove any dirt. Place them in a kettle with boiling salted water, and cook them until they are tender, approximately 15 to 20 minutes.

    Drain the potatoes well, and place them on a serving plate. Top the potatoes with a dollop of *crème fraîche* and then with a smaller dollop of caviar.

Purée of Wild Mushroom Soup

For this soup you may substitute other mushrooms—cepes, morels, or shiitake for the dried, and chanterelles or crimini for the fresh. Sometimes I combine two or three kinds of fresh mushrooms. Whatever combination you use, you cannot go wrong.

1 ounce dried porcini
   mushrooms
1 cup Madeira wine
½ cup (¼ pound) unsalted
   butter
1 small onion, chopped fine
2 garlic cloves, minced
2 leeks, white part only,
   chopped fine
1 small baking potato,
   chopped fine

1 pound fresh shiitake
   mushrooms, chopped
3 cups chicken stock
3 cups beef stock
Fresh-ground pepper to taste
Crème fraîche (see page 31)
4 scallions, sliced thin
   diagonally

In a sieve, rinse the porcini mushrooms. Set them aside.

In a small saucepan, bring the Madeira to a boil. Remove the pan from the heat, add the porcini mushrooms, and let them stand for 30 minutes. Drain the mushrooms in a paper towel–lined sieve, reserving the liquid in a bowl underneath. Chop the mushrooms coarsely.

In a kettle, melt the butter. Add the onion, garlic, leeks, and potato, and cook until the vegetables are soft, stirring occasionally, for 15 minutes. Add the fresh shiitake mushrooms to the kettle, and cook until they are softened, stirring occasionally, about 10 minutes. Add the chicken and beef stocks, the reserved porcini mushrooms, and the reserved soaking liquid, and bring the mixture to a boil. Reduce the heat, and simmer the mixture, partially covered, for 30 minutes.

Purée the soup, in batches, in a blender or a food processor. Return the soup to the kettle, and reheat it over low heat. Season it generously with pepper.

Ladle the soup into bowls and garnish with small dollops of *crème fraîche* and with the sliced scallions.

Serves 6

Tenderloin of Beef with Horseradish Sauce

I always roast our beef tenderloins this way, and they come out perfect every time.

The sauce was inspired by Ted's habit of putting horseradish on his leftover beef sandwiches. Why not in a sauce? I thought.

2 tablespoons unsalted
   butter
2 tablespoons onion, minced
   fine
½ cup red wine vinegar
¼ cup cognac
½ cup beef stock
½ cup chicken stock
1 cup heavy cream

¼ cup prepared horseradish,
   drained
Fresh-ground pepper to taste
3 pounds beef tenderloin,
   trimmed, at room
   temperature
3 tablespoons olive oil
Salt to taste
Fresh broccoli, steamed

In a saucepan, melt the butter. Add the onion, and cook over medium-low heat, stirring, until the onion is softened, about 5 minutes. Add the vinegar and cognac, and boil the mixture until it is reduced to ¼ cup. Add both stocks, and boil the mixture until it is reduced by one-half. Add the cream, and gently boil until the mixture is again reduced by one-half. Add the horseradish and pepper to the sauce, and keep the sauce warm.

Preheat the oven to 500°. Rub the tenderloin with the olive oil, sprinkle it with salt and pepper, and place it in a roasting pan. Roast the tenderloin for 25 minutes (for medium-rare meat). Transfer the roast to a cutting board, and let it stand, covered loosely with foil, for 15 minutes.

Slice the tenderloin, arrange the slices on individual plates, top with the horseradish sauce, and serve with the steamed broccoli.

Serves 8

Chocolate Mousse Rum Cake

This dessert takes time, but the results are well worth it. You can make the *génoise* ahead of time and either refrigerate it for a couple of days, or freeze it, wrapped first in plastic, then in foil. The *crème anglaise* can be made one day ahead and kept covered in the refrigerator.

FOR THE *GÉNOISE*:
⅓ cup unsalted butter
1 cup sugar
5 eggs, at room temperature

5 egg yolks, at room temperature
1 cup cake flour, sifted

FOR THE MOUSSE:
1 pound semisweet chocolate, chopped
1 cup milk
½ cup sugar
6 egg yolks, at room temperature

1 pound unsalted butter, at room temperature, cut into pieces
2 cups heavy cream

FOR THE ASSEMBLY:
6 tablespoons light rum

FOR THE *CRÈME ANGLAISE*:
4 egg yolks, at room temperature
½ cup sugar

2 cups heavy cream
2 tablespoons light rum

Prepare the *génoise:* Butter the bottom and side of a 10-inch springform pan. Line the bottom of the pan with parchment paper, and flour the side.

In a small pan, melt the butter, and keep it warm.

Preheat the oven to 300°.

Bring 2 inches of water to a gentle boil in a wide, deep saucepan. In the bowl of an electric mixer, whisk together the sugar, eggs, and egg yolks. Place the bowl over, but not touching, the boiling water. Whisk the mixture just until it is hot. Transfer the bowl to the electric mixer, and whip the mixture at high speed until it has doubled in volume. Beat it at medium speed for 2 additional minutes.

Sprinkle the flour over the batter, and gently fold it in. Gently fold in the melted butter.

Immediately pour the batter into the prepared springform pan. Bake the cake 1 hour, or until the center springs back when lightly touched and the *génoise* is light brown. Let the cake cool in the pan for 10 minutes, then remove the side of the pan. Invert the cake onto a wire rack, remove the bottom of the pan and the parchment paper, and invert the cake again onto another wire rack. Let the cake cool.

Prepare the mousse: In the top of a double boiler, combine the chocolate, milk, sugar, and egg yolks. In the bottom of the double boiler, bring 2 inches of water to a simmer. Set the top of the double boiler over the bottom. With a wire whisk, beat the chocolate mixture constantly until the chocolate is melted, then remove the entire double boiler from the heat. Continue beating the chocolate until it is thickened. Remove the top of the double boiler from the bottom.

Continue beating the mixture while adding the butter, one piece at a time. Beat until all the butter has been melted and incorporated and the mixture is quite thick.

Beat the heavy cream until it is stiff, and fold it into the chocolate mixture.

Assemble the cake: Place the *génoise* on a flat surface. Using the bottom of a 9-inch pan as a form, cut off 1 inch around the edge of the *génoise*. Set the crumbs and cut-off pieces aside. Using a serrated knife, cut horizontally through the 9-inch *génoise* to make two layers.

Place the bottom half of the *génoise*, cut side up, in a 9-inch springform pan. With a pastry brush, brush 3 tablespoons of light rum over the *génoise*. Spread one-third of the chocolate mousse mixture over the *génoise*.

Lay the top of the *génoise*, cut side down, over the chocolate mousse layer. Brush the remaining 3 tablespoons of light rum over the second *génoise* layer. Spread one-half of the remaining chocolate mousse mixture on the second cake layer.

Refrigerate the cake and the remaining mousse mixture for 4 hours. Then release the sides of the springform pan, and place the cake on a serving platter. Spread the remaining chocolate mousse mixture evenly around the sides of the cake.

Crumble the reserved *génoise* pieces. Press the crumbs gently on the sides of the cake so they adhere.

Make the *crème anglaise*: In a small bowl, whisk together the egg yolks and sugar thoroughly.

In a heavy saucepan, heat the heavy cream just until it comes to a boil. Whisk half the cream into the egg yolk mixture, then add all the egg yolk–cream mixture to the saucepan. Cook the mixture, stirring constantly, over low heat, until it is thickened and coats the back of a spoon. Be sure the custard does not come to a boil.

Pour the custard into a bowl, and set the bowl over ice, stirring constantly until the custard is cool. Stir in the rum, and refrigerate the *crème anglaise*.

Cut the cake into wedges, and serve it on plates with the *crème anglaise* on the side.

Serves 12

SEAFOOD DINNER

Crab Cakes with Roasted Red Pepper Sauce

Oyster Bisque

Ragout of Lobster

Apple Pie

FOR THE FRESHEST SEAFOOD possible, there's no place like the coast of Maine. Lobsters from Maine are shipped all over the world. I remember seeing fresh Maine lobster featured as a special in the dining room at the airport in St. Maarten. When we were in California, Maine lobster was the *pièce de résistance* on many a menu. I did not acquire a taste for lobster until just a couple of years ago, when I first ate one that was really fresh. I am a big fan now.

Lobster isn't the only Maine seafood that's shipped all over the world. The Japanese are big buyers of Maine shrimp and sea-urchin roe. Right here on the Damariscotta River is an oyster farm. At the Grand Central Station Raw Bar in New York, some of the most popular oysters are those raised right here on our river. Wonderful clams are also being farmed near us.

At our inn, we do not normally serve lobster, because too many people are allergic to it. We are more than happy, however, to steam a lobster on request as an alternative entrée. We also serve crab, oysters, scallops, and other seafood for our first and soup courses.

With its three kinds of seafood and apple pie, I think of this menu as my Maine dinner. The menu would be especially wonderful for a dinner party during the holiday season, when oysters are at their peak. The elegant Lobster Ragout would be the hit of the party.

Crab Cakes with Roasted Red Pepper Sauce

I love the combination of the crab cakes and the roasted red pepper sauce. The crab cakes are also good with a dollop of *crème fraîche*, a light tomato sauce, or *aioli* (garlic mayonnaise). Or you can serve them plain.

4 large red bell peppers, roasted, peeled, cored, seeded, and cut into ½-inch strips
5 tablespoons olive oil
2 garlic cloves, minced
Salt and pepper to taste
1 small onion, diced
2 tablespoons Dijon mustard
1 tablespoon Worcestershire sauce
3 tablespoons chopped Italian parsley

⅛ teaspoon cayenne pepper
2 drops Tabasco sauce
½ teaspoon fresh-ground black pepper
1 egg, lightly beaten
2 tablespoons heavy cream
1 cup fresh bread crumbs
1½ pounds fresh crab meat
2 tablespoons unsalted butter

Make the sauce: Combine the red peppers, 2 tablespoons olive oil, and garlic in a food processor, and purée. Add salt and pepper. Transfer the sauce to a small saucepan, and set it aside.

Make the crab cakes: Heat 1 tablespoon olive oil in a large skillet. Add the onion, and sauté it until it is soft, about 5 minutes. Transfer the onion mixture to a large bowl, and let it cool.

Add to the onion mixture the mustard, Worcestershire sauce, parsley, cayenne pepper, Tabasco sauce, and ½ teaspoon black pepper. Stir the mixture well to combine the ingredients. Stir in the egg, heavy cream, and bread crumbs. Gently fold in the crab meat.

Line a baking sheet with parchment paper. Shape the mixture into 12 patties, and place them on the baking sheet. Refrigerate the patties, covered, for 2 to 4 hours.

In a large skillet, melt the butter and the remaining 2 tablespoons olive oil. Add six crab cakes, and sauté them over medium-high heat until they are golden brown, about 3 minutes on each side. Remove the patties to a shallow pan, and set them aside in a warm oven. Sauté the remaining patties in the skillet, using additional olive oil if needed.

Warm the roasted red pepper sauce over low heat.

Divide the sauce among six plates, place two crab cakes on top of the sauce on each plate, and serve at once.

Serves 6

Oyster Bisque

Oysters are traditionally eaten during the Thanksgiving and Christmas holidays, but this soup could be served anytime.

Pinch salt
1 pound spinach, leaves only, washed and drained
4 tablespoons unsalted butter
4 leeks, white part only, chopped fine
½ pound mushrooms, chopped fine
Rind of 1 lemon, grated fine

1 cup dry white wine
1 quart shucked oysters, in their own liquid
2 tablespoons chopped Italian parsley
2 cups heavy cream
4 cups light cream
Fresh-ground black pepper to taste
Fresh-ground nutmeg

In a saucepan, heat 2 cups water with the pinch of salt. When the water comes to a boil, add the spinach leaves. Stir to immerse all the leaves. Bring the water to a boil again, and simmer the spinach 5 minutes. Immediately transfer the pan to the sink and run cold water into it. Transfer the spinach to a strainer. Press with the back of a spoon to extract as much liquid as possible.

Melt the butter in a kettle. Add the leeks, and cook them over medium heat until they are soft, about 5 minutes.

Add the mushrooms to the leek mixture, and sauté for 3 minutes. Add the lemon rind and white wine, and bring the mixture to a boil. Add the spinach to the mixture, and bring to a boil again. Add the oysters and their liquid, and cook only until the edges of the oysters start to curl, about 5 minutes.

Remove the kettle from the heat, and let the mixture cool slightly. In a food processor, pulse the mixture only to chop it. Do not purée it.

Return the soup to the kettle. Add the parsley and heavy and light creams, and heat over low heat. Season with pepper.

Serve the soup at once, garnished with a sprinkling of nutmeg.

Serves 6

Ragout of Lobster

Although this dish is a lot more work than just steaming lobster, it is well worth the effort.

2 1½-pound lobsters
¼ pound plus 3 tablespoons
    unsalted butter
3 leeks, white part only,
    chopped fine
1 garlic clove, minced
10 ounces peeled Italian
    tomatoes, drained and
    coarsely chopped
¾ cup dry white wine

2 tablespoons tomato paste
1 small onion, minced
2 tablespoons white wine
    vinegar
¼ cup heavy cream
⅓ cup cognac
Salt and fresh-ground pepper
    to taste
Boiled rice

In a large kettle, bring 2 inches of salted water to a boil. Plunge the lobsters into the kettle, cover the kettle, and steam the lobsters for 13 to 15 minutes, until they have turned red. Transfer the lobsters to a bowl, reserving the cooking liquid. Let the lobsters cool slightly, then cut off the claws, and remove the meat. Split the underside of the tail shell lengthwise, and remove the tail meat. Cut the tail meat into four pieces; keep the claw meat whole.

In a skillet, melt 2 tablespoons of the butter. Add the leeks and garlic, and sauté them until they are soft, about 5 minutes. Add the tomatoes, ½ cup of the white wine, and 2 tablespoons of the reserved cooking liquid. Bring the mixture to a boil, reduce the heat, and cook for 15 minutes, or until the mixture is thick. Add the tomato paste, and stir well. Keep the tomato mixture warm.

In a small saucepan, combine the onion, the remaining ¼ cup white wine, the white wine vinegar, and ¼ cup reserved lobster liquid. Bring the mixture to a boil, and boil until it is reduced to ¼ cup. Whisk in the heavy cream, and boil until the mixture is again reduced to ¼ cup.

Cut ¼ pound butter into small pieces. Whisk the butter into the mixture, one piece at a time. Set the sauce aside.

In a skillet, melt the remaining 1 tablespoon butter. Add the lobster meat, season with salt and pepper, and heat gently for 2 to 3 minutes. Add the cognac, and ignite it by touching a lit match to the edge of the skillet. Remove the skillet from the heat.

Divide the boiled rice among four plates. Spoon the tomato mixture over the rice. Spoon the lobster over the tomato mixture, and top with the sauce.

Serves 4

Apple Pie

If any dessert has "New England" written all over it, this is it. Apple pie warm from the oven is Ted's favorite dessert. I use Northern Spy apples or a combination of MacIntoshes and Cortlands.

FOR THE PASTRY:

1 tablespoon apple cider
  vinegar
½ teaspoon salt

2 cups all-purpose flour
1 cup plus 2 tablespoons
  shortening

FOR THE FILLING:

2½ pounds apples
1 tablespoon lemon juice
1 teaspoon ground cinnamon
½ teaspoon ground nutmeg
1½ tablespoons all-purpose
  flour

6 tablespoons sugar
3 tablespoons unsalted
  butter, cut into small
  pieces

Make the pastry: In a small bowl, blend together the vinegar, the salt, and ⅓ cup water.

In a large bowl, cut the shortening into the flour until the mixture resembles cornmeal. With a fork, lightly blend in the liquid, a little at a time. Gather the dough into a ball, wrap it in plastic, and refrigerate it for 15 minutes.

Divide the dough in half. Roll one piece of the dough into a 12-inch circle, and lay it in a 9-inch pie pan. Refrigerate the dough in the pan.

Preheat the oven to 425°.

Peel, core, and slice the apples, and put the slices in a bowl. Add the lemon juice, spices, flour, and sugar, and toss the mixture. Arrange the apples in the pastry-lined pan to fill it evenly, making a dome in the center. Dot with the butter.

Roll out the remaining pastry, and lay it on top of the pie. Press the two dough edges together, trim them, and crimp them. Cut four steam vents in the top of the pie.

Place the pie in the center of the oven, and immediately

reduce the temperature to 400°. Bake the pie 45 to 50 minutes, or until the crust is browned and the apples are juicy.

Serve the pie warm with vanilla ice cream.

Serves 8

INDEX

ABOUT THE AUTHOR:
Chris Sprague and her husband, Ted, have been welcoming guests at their inn since 1987. Their enthusiasm for innkeeping and passion for food have made the Newcastle Inn a destination for lovers of exceptional cuisine in a relaxed setting.

ABOUT THE ILLUSTRATOR:
Joanna Roy studied at California State University, Long Beach, and at Barnard College, Parsons, the School of Visual Arts, and the Art Students League in New York. Her scratchboard illustrations appear in the *New York Times* and other newspapers, in *Travel and Leisure* and other magazines, and in books and calendars. She lives in New York.